ICHTHYOLOGY
AND
OTOLITHS

ICHTHYOLOGY AND OTOLITHS

My Life as a Foreign Fisheries Observer

Neva Dail Bridges

Library of Congress Number: 2004091552
ISBN :   Softcover   1-4134-5071-7

To order additional copies of this book, contact:
Xlibris Corporation
1-888-795-4274
www.Xlibris.com
Orders@Xlibris.com
23801

This book is dedicated to my friends and family
who encouraged me to tell my story, and
who helped me to craft it so that reading it will,
I hope, be as enticing to you as living it was to me.

And to Valerya, wherever he may be, who taught me
much about courage, love and loyalty.

CONTENTS

One: Jacob's Ladder 9

Two: Intro to Chin Barbels 13

Three: Kyowa Maru 22

Four: Table Manners 32

Five: Fishing 41

Six: Secret Codes 54

Seven: Man Overboard 62

Eight: My Fair Lady 67

Nine: Orekhova 82

Ten: Tea, Compot, and Spy Work 97

Eleven: Hide and Seek 113

Twelve: Propaganda and Peanut Butter 126

Thirteen: Cabin Search 132

Fourteen: Galley Fight 143

Fifteen: Fear 150

Sixteen: The Captain's Dinner Party 155

Seventeen: KGB 162

Eighteen: New Year's Eve 169

Nineteen: Valerya 185

Epilogue 197

ONE

Jacob's Ladder

THE SEAS HAD CALMED. THE WAVES IN THE HARBOR CRESTED AT heights of only eight to ten feet, in stark contrast to the earlier towering walls of water that had slammed through the bay. For four days, Alaska winter winds had roared between the mountains that encircled Dutch Harbor, this small fishing village in the middle of the Aleutian Island chain.

After my third day of motel room confinement, I had attempted to walk down the snow banked, ice-chunked strip that passed for the main street of this frozen town. The cold had seared into me. My bulky layers of clothing offered no more protection than a light windbreaker. I'd bowed my head and narrowed my eyes, determined to breathe fresh air. That's what you do where I'm from. In North Carolina, when you've been cooped up, you go for a walk. Somehow, the physical impact of the climate difference between North Carolina and Alaska had eluded me until this point.

I had slogged on, my throat burning with every intake of frigid air. My fingers turned numb and I couldn't feel my toes. I shivered all over. I'd been walking for perhaps three minutes, and I had never known anything like this. I'd thought of the south, where, even in February, the end of winter begins its roll into spring. And how that springtime comes effortlessly, the chill of the winter season simply fading away as the days and nights fill up with warmth and sweet fragrances. The harshness of this world had frightened me; I couldn't imagine this place ever being soft, or filled with anything other than killing winds and snow banks the size of dinosaurs. I'd turned back, suddenly desperate for the safety of my lonely room.

Snug again in my heated cocoon, I'd watched the turmoil of the sea—huge waves pounding and crashing, mixed with swirling snow and ice.

But now the weather had broken. There was no getting around it; the time had come to go. I stood on the upper dock in the harbor, gazing down at the small pilot boat below me. The door to the wheelhouse flew open and a weathered face peered out.

"Whatcha' waiting for? That Jap boat won't stick around all day just for you. Get on down here and let's go!" His voice was stern, but the skipper grinned as he looked up at me.

Dragging my gear baskets and duffel bag, I struggled to reach the boat that would take me to meet my Japanese fishing trawler. I threw the stack of gear baskets onto the back of the tugboat. These blue plastic baskets were standard issue for all foreign fisheries observers and, like ankle shackles that could not be removed, we lugged them everywhere.

I hoisted the overstuffed duffel bag onto my back and immediately collapsed under its weight. There went my plan to jump with it, piggyback style, down onto the boat. I rolled out from under the barge-like pack and dragged it to the side of the dock. The pilot boat bobbed about four feet below me. I positioned the duffel, imagining it a cannon ready to fire, and rushed at it, shoving with all my strength. The misshapen cannon ball, lacking true firepower, tilted slightly and finally sagged over the edge, flopping onto the deck below.

I followed the duffel, and a dock worker unleashed the boat. We leapt away from the wooden pilings, pitching and bouncing, a wild animal finally freed from its tethers. One minute I was on a solid wooden platform; the next I was jettisoning through space on a roller coaster, with no safety belts to strap me in. Unable to stand, I crawled toward the front of the boat. Grasping the door to the wheelhouse, I jerked it open, just as a large swell heaved us upwards. As I tumbled onto the bridge, we nose-dived sharply into the trough of the wave.

"Yep, looks like it's going to be a rough one today." The pilot grimaced as he puffed on his cigarette. "This your first time out?"

"You mean it's not obvious?" I gasped, struggling to keep my balance as the boat's motions threatened to throw me to my knees.

The pilot laughed. "Come to think of it, you do look a little green. Agh, you fishery observers! There's a bucket tied up under the bench there if you need to puke. Just don't get any on the control panel here." He patted the console beside him. "Usually we try to do these transfers when it's a little calmer, but this break in the storm might be our only chance. This mess is due to kick up again tonight."

As I scrambled on my hands and knees for the bucket, the pilot said he thought he saw my boat up ahead. He peered through the rain-drenched window and asked me what the call letters were. At this point, I could barely remember my name, much less the call sign for a vessel I'd never seen. I mumbled something to that effect, but the grizzled seaman didn't seem to hear me.

"Looks like it says 7LPS . . . can't quite make out that name . . . *Kyowa Maru* number 13 . . . no, that's 15—this has gotta be your boat; we don't have any other Japs scheduled to be in the harbor. Now this is gonna to be a bit tricky here—gotta pull up beside her real careful. Holy Christ, look at the size of those waves!" The pilot battled to maneuver the boat alongside the 150-foot *Kyowa Maru.*

I was zipping up my raincoat and struggling to put on my life jacket, as well as trying to remain upright and, most importantly, not throw up. I desperately wanted to crawl to a corner, curl into a ball and wake from this nightmare, back on solid ground, these nauseating gyrations a thing of the past. Instead, the pilot gave me a gentle push out of the wheelhouse and onto the deck. The wind blasted me, and I leaned into it to keep from being forced backwards.

The crew of the *Kyowa Maru* lowered a jacob's ladder down the side of their ship. The soggy wooden steps, joined with knotted ropes, whipped against the hull as we bobbed beside the taller ship. I looked down into the narrow space that separated the two vessels, into the wildly churning waves that crashed over the deck, drenching me with freezing spray. I thought of falling, and what it would be like to be smashed between tons of metal. The cold would probably kill me first.

The veteran of sea transfers put his hands around my waist and shouted over the wind, "Ya gotta climb up on the edge—you can't jump from here!" He tried to lift me up onto the deck railing. I must have carried an additional 20 pounds in foul weather gear. My life jacket imprisoned me, bound tightly around me like a straight jacket. My arms dangled uselessly, heavy as lead weights. Like tree trunks, my legs remained rooted in place. Hoisting myself up onto the railing seemed impossible.

The cursing pilot, practiced in the ways of terrified observers, struggled and shoved until I perched on the edge. He leaned against me, steadying me from behind. When we seemed to be on top of a wave, I forced myself to leap through the air, slamming into the side of the *Kyowa*. Miraculously, I managed to grab the ladder. I quickly hauled myself up a few steps, the pilot boat leaping behind me like a monster from the deep, and missing me by inches.

Breathing in great, jagged gasps, gulping in air, I clung to the wildly twisting ladder. Then I forced myself to inch upward, rolling first to the left and then to the right as the ladder swung crazily with the movement of the boat. Finally, I reached the top and clambered over the railing onto the deck of the Japanese ship. I looked down to see the pilot boat, bouncing like a cork, pulling away from the *Kyowa* to head back to shore.

I thought how unreal this all seemed. What was I doing, standing on the deck of a Japanese fishing trawler, in the dead of an Alaskan winter, heading out for two months into the middle of the Bering Sea?

TWO

Intro to Chin Barbels

IN 1983 I COMPLETED A BACHELOR'S DEGREE IN PSYCHOLOGY AT THE University of North Carolina at Chapel Hill. I went to work in a group home for severely emotionally disturbed adolescents in a small coastal town in North Carolina and I lived with my parents.

And I was restless. North Carolina was too small for me. I had lived all over the state, but still I wanted a life bigger than me, bigger than what the South, with all of its heritage and traditions, expected of me. All of my growing up years had been spent here— it was what I knew and what I was comfortable with—and what I was most afraid of. Every time a woman friend of mine announced her engagement or told me she was pregnant, I felt panic. Please, no, not me—don't let this end up being me.

As my friends disappeared into their quiet, suburban lives, I seemed more and more a stranger to them. When I spoke of traveling to far off places, of my yearning to explore the world, they would stare at me, incredulous. The uncomfortable silence would be broken with a question about my family or a comment about the weather. The weight of tradition and expectation was smothering. I would explode if I did not get out.

Then I met Victoria, a woman who lived outside the mold. She was a marine biologist and she cruised all over the world on research vessels. When I met her, Vic was working for a scientist at Duke University's Marine Laboratory. Her job was to take her on a two-month cruise on the NOAA (National Oceanic and Atmospheric Administration) ship, the *Discoverer*, in the equatorial South Pacific. But she could do only one leg of the trip and needed a substitute for the second month. With the proper training, Vic assured me, I could easily take her place. I happily left my job and the teenagers who were intent on killing me, each other, and themselves. Vic arranged it so that the lab would fly me down to Manzanillo, Mexico to meet and board the *Disco* and she would return home.

All that remained was for Vic to train me to do the research and—did we think this would be easy?—teach me how to be a scientist. The research scientists on these cruises were a competitive bunch. They would kill for data, not to mention run roughshod over an impostor in their midst. Vic warned me that I must enact the full charade; if any of these cutthroats had even an inkling that I was not who I pretended to be, they would make my life miserable. She recounted tales of passive researchers being "forgotten" or not awakened so that they failed to collect data at certain work stations; others who missed out on computer-processed data because they were too shy to ask for it. We trained together for two weeks, until Vic convinced me that I could carry off the deception without a hitch.

Working on the *Disco* was my first taste of being at sea, and I loved it. I'd spent much of my life exploring the marshes and islands of the North Carolina coast. Summertime, early mornings, I would set off in tattered shorts and musty tennis shoes, wading through the tall grasses and shallow waters of the nearby inlets, searching for treasures uncovered by low tide. Startled blue herons would rise before me, like ungainly elephants struggling to take flight. Low country smells of salt and marsh grass filled the air. I would lose myself for hours, mesmerized by the dance of sunlight on silver water. The South Pacific was warm and soft, as my summers on the Atlantic coast had been, and it nurtured me. I felt safe, surrounded by these vast, calm waters. I loved waking early every morning and rushing out onto the open deck, breathing deeply of the fresh ocean smell, gazing across the endless blue water. Whenever a whale or porpoise broke the surface of the glassy sea, I gratefully accepted the special gift—a personal show, meant only for me.

Amazingly, I managed to blend in with all of the real-life

scientists on the *Disco*, working side by side with them and never arousing suspicion. One of the researchers especially intrigued me, a marine bird specialist named Larry Spears. Larry previously had been a foreign fisheries observer with the Pacific Northwest program and had worked in Alaska. He regaled me for hours with his stories of adventure on the, literally, high seas. I hung on his every word, asking endless questions. Through Larry's stories, I started to envision what it must be like to work on a foreign fishing boat in the cold waters north of Alaska. Recognizing my keen interest, he urged me to apply to the program in Seattle, if I really wanted to work in the Bering Sea. And I finally confessed my secret to Larry.

"Right, Larry—me and my B.A. in psychology. I am sure the Foreign Fisheries Observer Program would happily hire a candidate without a degree in marine biology or even simple biology." I could not imagine anything less likely.

Larry explained that there was a high demand for observers because most only do the job once. At any one time, dozens of foreign vessels needed observers on board, as it was illegal to fish in American waters without one. The program needed a steady supply of new people to fill observer positions. Besides, he said, I had done what appeared to be an excellent job with my research work on the *Disco*—working as an observer would be a piece of cake.

We pulled into Seattle in November, and I requested an application from Larry's contractor, Oregon State University. I returned to North Carolina, and when the foreign fisheries observer application arrived, I read and re-read the questions.

"What courses have you had in the field of biology? Marine biology? What field work have you done that would apply to fisheries? To this position specifically? Have you had at least one course in ichthyology?"

I had to look up the word ichthyology. "Ichthyology: a branch of zoology dealing with fishes," revealed page 244 of my old Webster's dictionary.

The only thing that I could come up with that was the least bit relevant from college were my two required statistics courses. I didn't mention that I had struggled terribly with both of them. In fact, I had given the second course a practice run by auditing it before taking it for a grade. Even then, the grade was miserably low. Thankfully I had something substantial to put under "Relevant Work Experience." My month of data collection and research on the *Disco* took up a full page of the application. I wondered if this would be positive or negative, as it certainly seemed to magnify the lack of any other experience. Mailing off the completed application, I decided not to hold my breath waiting for a response.

When an envelope arrived from Oregon in early January, the first thing I noticed was its thinness. I envisioned the enclosed rejection letter: "Thank you for applying to be a foreign fisheries observer, but we suggest you look for work within your field of psychology. For observer positions, we hire those individuals who have some degree of training in the biological sciences."

Already feeling disappointment, I tore open the envelope to read: "Your application to be a foreign fisheries observer has been accepted. Please report to Seattle, Washington for a two-week training course beginning February 8, 1984 . . . ."

Later, I would find out that the federal government had just mandated that observer coverage of foreign ships be 100%. And, per the government contract of Oregon State University, they were required to supply the majority of people for this new coverage rate. My timing was perfect.

Next began the flurry of getting organized to go to Seattle. What to take? What not to take? The Bering Sea . . . Alaska . . . both conjured up mental images of icebergs and impenetrable mountain peaks. My days of winter camping in the North Carolina Blue Ridge Mountains paid off, and I piled together hats, gloves, long underwear, and wool sweaters and socks. An army duffel bag barely contained my belongings. I emptied out my meager savings account and purchased a plane ticket to Seattle. All, I felt, was in order for my departure in three weeks.

*   *   *

Day one of the Foreign Fisheries Observer Training Course in

Seattle found about 30 of us gathered in a classroom at the Naval Reserve Center on the shores of Lake Union.

The trainer asked each of us to stand and introduce ourselves and discuss our background. It quickly became evident that I was surrounded by people from all over the country who had graduate degrees in ichthyology, marine biology, fisheries management and/ or extensive experience in these fields.

My nervous imagination threatened to take over. I imagined this as the first session of group therapy. Perhaps an Alcoholics Anonymous meeting. I would be forced to stand, raise my right hand and state, "My name is Dail Bridges. I am a Pretend Scientist. Only a month ago I did not know what ichthyology meant. I am an impostor—the worst kind. I am turning myself over to this group—do with me as you will."

Interrupted from my flight by the instructor, I stood, recited my name and actually said, "I'm a graduate of the University of North Carolina at Chapel Hill and recently worked for a month on the NOAA ship *Discoverer*, gathering data for research on El Nino." I sat back down, hoping no one would ask any questions and, most of all, that the trainer wouldn't say, "What did you say your degree was in?" I was safe. The person next to me immediately stood up, eliminating any chance for queries.

After introductions, the trainer gave us an overview of the course and what was expected of us as foreign fisheries observers. We would be taught specific scientific sampling techniques with which we would determine the species composition of each catch our boat brought on board, as well as methods of estimating the total size of each catch. We would learn fish and crab identification and identification of certain protected species (various halibut, salmon and king crab) that the foreign ships were not allowed to retain, because they were reserved for American fishing boats. Americans are such picky eaters that of all of the fish in the Bering Sea, these were the only ones with a market in the States.

A whole session would be devoted to collecting otoliths and length frequencies from certain species. I leaned toward my neighbor and inquired in a whisper, wondering what otoliths were. Fish earbones, I was told. Fish earbones? I tried to picture a fish with ears. Did they have earlobes? Perhaps some even had pierced ears, a glittery stud embedded in their slimy flesh. Surely the Pretend Scientist was going to be found out. I could never pull this off.

To record our data, we would have to learn the intricacies of 11 different and very detailed data forms. We would also go over life at sea, safety and emergency procedures and interactions with a foreign culture. Training on fisheries regulation and enforcement, as well as our role in this area, would entail a full day. Marine mammal identification was to complete the course.

I wallowed in my own sea of confusion. The very language the trainer used sounded like a foreign tongue. Otoliths, chin barbels, ventral fins, sculpins, Greenland turbot. My brain reeled with the amount of statistical and mathematical work, and work in general, that would be required on the job. I had entertained visions of throwing a few fish around, scouting with binoculars for marine mammals, and, perhaps, some paperwork for documentation purposes. My visions, it turned out, were wildly inaccurate. It was bad enough feeling intimidated by the caliber of people around me; now I wasn't sure I was even capable of doing the job. I reminded myself that I had just spent a month working with people who assumed I was a marine scientist.

As class progressed, the instructor shared stories from past observers ("priors," as the program referred to them). We heard of elaborate cheating systems boats set up to throw off observers' calculations. Tales of working in the factory day and night, of endless piles of fish, of food so bad everyone on the ship became ill. Drunken crews who staggered to work when a trawl came on.

One prior returned from sea as our class was in session with a tale that disturbed us all. His Japanese trawler collided with another one in heavy seas and sustained minimal damage, but the second one sank. This observer had participated in an intense rescue operation that was only partially successful; 14 men went down with the ship. Like passengers scheduled on an airline whose jet had just crashed, we could not resist the news of the disaster. We clustered around Tom, demanding that he share every detail of his nightmare.

Ironically, the training schedule called for survival suit drills the next morning. We entered our training room to find a large stack of heavy canvas bags piled in a corner. Our instructor issued each of us a sack, which contained a standard, one-size-fits-all survival suit. Huge orange insulated affairs, the suits were to be pulled on over our clothes and zipped up tightly. If an emergency found us heading into the water, the suit design should keep us dry and warm. The instructor held a Gumby-like suit up in front of the class and pointed out the features: a small air hose that inflated a ring around your neck to help you float; a whistle that dangled from one shoulder—the instructor insisted that its shrill sound could be heard over thunderous waves and shrieking winds; a dynamite-sized flare nestling under the deflated neck ring that ignited when you pulled it sharply forward and off the suit. The instructor assured us that even using an arm weakened by shock and cold, we could throw the flare as far as necessary to attract the attention of nearby rescue vessels.

The feature demonstration completed, the instructor casually mentioned that a ship can sink in four minutes. He shouted a command and clicked a stop watch as we raced to put on our suits. The room filled with the sounds of ripping Velcro as we pulled open our storage bags. I yanked my suit out, rolling it onto the floor. Suits were always stored unzipped, so I thrust my steel-toed boots (again, standard issue) into the leg holes and sat on the floor. The polyurethane squeaked and stuck along my boots, resisting my tugging. My left boot jammed in the knee fold. I twisted and shoved, lying flat on the floor and raising my tangled left leg in the air. Nothing worked. I shook off the suit. My hands quivered, lacking the strength to try, once again, to pull the suit over my boots. Sweat rolled down my face and dampened my clothes. I breathed deeply to calm my racing heart.

One-liners flew back and forth among my classmates:

"Hey, maybe we can market these as giant sausage holders!"

"Are we supposed to be able to *move* in these things, or just roll around on the floor?"

"Joan, you've got *your* leg in *my* arm hole!"

Though my classmates laughed and joked, tension hung in the air. We all understood how serious the situation would be if we had to put these on at sea. I was warm, dry and on solid ground and still my suit defeated me. I could not imagine what it would be like trying this on a storm-rocked ship in the Bering Sea.

After class that day, I wandered the shore of Lake Union, huddled in my wool sweater and gortex jacket, plodding along in the cold rain. I thought about Tom, the shipwreck survivor, wondering what it felt like to be faced with the possibility of going down at sea. He had related only the physical details of his experience. We had not allowed him to share his emotions with us; there had been no room for this.

I had buried my fear in a deep, hidden place. Sometimes, pieces of it would creep out and startle me with their strength. I closed my eyes, seeing men tumbling around on the flooded deck of a ship, grasping and missing at hand-holds, sliding into the water as the boat upended into the churning ocean. I remembered sweating on the cool linoleum floor of the training class, my survival suit hopelessly tangled around my knees.

I *could* leave class. The trainer reiterated daily that this was an option; if any of us felt uncomfortable or unable, we were free to leave at any time. But what would I do? Where would I go? I watched the Canada Geese paddling on the lake and thought of North Carolina. The rain pelted my face as I shook my head. This job meant my escape from that world. It was my ticket out. Not only that, but to return home would mean defeat. I would feel like I had quit before I even started. Besides, I wanted to surround myself with people who were totally different from me. Who talked, ate, and thought in a way I did not know. I flashed again on the smallness of my world, the sameness of the people who had always filled it. I knew I could not go back.

By the end of the training course, five people had dropped out. They gave various reasons, not the least of which was fear of being in a dangerous environment. (Three of the five left the day after the survival suit drill.) The trainer bestowed the remaining 25 of us with ship assignments, some Soviet, but mostly Japanese.

Which is how I found myself standing on the deck of a 150-foot long Japanese fishing trawler in the middle of winter, in the pouring rain and freezing cold of Dutch Harbor, Alaska.

THREE

Kyowa Maru

CHAOS ENGULFED ME. THE DECK OF THE JAPANESE BOAT WAS ALIVE with men in black rubber suits, scurrying like ants over piles of nets that seemed as if they would topple at any moment. The wind threatened to blow me back over the side. It filled my ears with a shrieking, like a vacuum cleaner with a live animal caught in its rollers. I spotted my duffel on the back of a man who matched it in size. The two staggered away from me, toward the enclosed front of the ship. A small man stood before me, mouthing words with no sound attached. I tried to wipe the icy rain from my eyes, shaking my head at him. He motioned for me to follow.

I stumbled over ropes and hoses, dangerous snakes coiled on the deck, trying to keep pace with the man in front of me. He yanked down, hard, on a handle in the white wall in front of us and pulled open the passageway door. I ducked my head and entered a dim hallway. Bending to pass through any doorway on this boat would soon become second nature. The passageways—and the ship overall—were designed not for my 5' 9" frame but for the shorter-statured Japanese men.

My guide slammed the door behind us, latching the handle into place. It was like entering a vacuum; the roaring wind was sealed off behind the solid door. My ears rang in the sudden silence. Warm air rushed against my face, the only exposed part of my body. The freezing rain outside had turned my eyelashes into thin, icy strips and now melting water droplets blurred my vision. I took a few steps after my guide, and he opened a tiny door, motioning me through.

I entered a rectangular room. If I stood in the middle of it and stretched my arms out, I could almost touch the walls on either side. I wondered why I had been led into a closet—then realized this was my cabin. Two bunks, well under six feet in length, were built along the wall opposite the doorway, about three giant steps from where I stood. Nestled into the wall on my left was a tiny metal desk with an even tinier stool tucked underneath. Beside it, also built into the wall, was a small wood paneled closet. A miniature sink, with a shiny mirror mounted above it, completed the furnishings in my cabin. There were no windows. The ceiling contained a three-foot plastic panel with fluorescent lights, which bathed the tiny space in a gray, artificial glow. The already dull gray metal walls looked even duller.

My duffel bag had miraculously appeared in the tiny doorway. Together my guide and I wrestled the huge barge into the cabin. We managed to get behind it, and, standing tightly wedged against each other, we hoisted it onto the top bunk. It lay like a beached walrus, taking up the entire bed. My guide said something in Japanese, pointed toward the ceiling, smiled, bowed slightly, and left me alone in the small, dim space that was to be my home for the next two months.

Protocol dictated that I meet the ships' officers as soon as possible. I wanted to get to the bridge, which is where I assumed they would be. But where *was* the bridge? And how to get there? And—oh, god—I had thought that being on a ship substantially larger than the pilot boat would calm my stomach. However, I still felt acutely the motions of the ship, and nausea threatened to overwhelm me. I struggled out of my rain jacket and life vest, pushing them into a corner of the room. I took a deep breath, opened my door and stepped tentatively out into the corridor.

To keep my mind off of my queasy stomach, I studied my surroundings. The chocolate brown linoleum floor cleverly disguised any dirt that might appear on its surface. Dull green metal walls stretched before me like an underground tunnel. The same feeble florescent light glowed over the area, and a faint unpleasant aroma permeated the ghostly hallway. Eventually this ubiquitous odor would become synonymous with the *Kyowa Maru*. Being enveloped by the combined smell of fish, diesel, cigarettes and fried food became simply a part of being on the ship.

The corridor throbbed quietly with the pulsing of the vessel. The dashing, frantic men of only minutes ago might have been a dream; I saw no one and heard no one. I had come in on the deck level, so I knew I had to go up to reach the bridge. Dozens of closed doors dotted the tunnel walls. Squiggly black Japanese characters danced on their surfaces. I felt off center and dizzy, like I was in a maze. Everything looked the same and wandering around only enhanced my disorientation. At last I heard laughter behind one of the doors and tentatively knocked on it. The door flew open and I stood face to face—actually, chest to face—with a five-foot tall man.

"Umm . . . excuse me, could you tell me where the bridge is?" I smiled politely.

A torrent of Japanese filled the tiny cabin. Various men sat cross-legged on the floor, dressed in pristine white long underwear. Through the cigarette haze, I saw two men pulling a chubby fellow to his feet. They dragged him to the doorway and placed him in front of me. He grinned hugely and his face shone like a rounded red apple.

"English! English!" several of the men shouted.

"Oh, do you speak English?" I almost collapsed with relief.

With great effort and many facial contortions, the gentleman replied, "I best English speak."

"Great! Where is the bridge? Can you take me to the bridge, or at least point me in the right direction?" I babbled happily along, only to be met with a totally blank stare. The fellows sitting around continued to laugh and prod at the man in front of me.

"Bridge," I pointed upward and made steering wheel motions.

"Ahhh!" The "English speaker" quickly stepped ahead of me, leading me down the corridor to one of the dozens of indistinguishable doorways I had previously passed. I tried to fix in my mind an image of the indecipherable black character on the door before my guide yanked it open. He pointed up the narrow stairway.

"*Arigato*!" I *had* learned how to say "thank you" in Japanese, which made my friend blush even more fiercely.

I climbed the dozen steps, my stomach rolling in time to the ship. I squinted as I emerged from the darkness into the daylight of the bridge; windows all around allowed the soft gray light of the overcast sky to fill the compact room. Instruments, humming and clicking mysteriously, packed every inch of space. Four men stood at the stern window smoking cigarettes. They turned at my unsteady approach, immediately looking at my feet. Perhaps they were too shy to look me in the eyes. I understood nothing of the excited chatter that streamed in my direction.

"*Ohayo Gozaimas*!" I managed to gasp out "good day" in Japanese, willing my churning stomach to remain calm. This greeting caused great guffaws of laughter among the men, but still their gazes remained fastened to my lower extremities. One of the men rushed forward and thrust a small pair of plastic sandals with inch high heels into my hands. They appeared to be about a size three.

"Miss, no shoes on bridge! Please, must use these! Please!" Agitated, the man literally jumped up and down.

Unable to stand any longer, I flopped heavily down onto the carpeted floor, embarrassed by my major breach of etiquette. Japanese never wear shoes indoors. House slippers or sandals only. I yanked at my heavy steel-toed boots, hurriedly trying to make amends. I managed to squeeze my toes and an inch more of my size ten feet into the tiny slippers. I tottered to my feet, now unbalanced not only by the rocking of the ship but also by my ridiculous footwear.

This shoe switch seemed to calm the men. A second one stepped forward, bowed and said "I captain."

"I . . . I . . . I am . . . I am going to throw up!!" I looked around for an open window, motioning wildly at my stomach.

One of the men appeared at my elbow with a trash can. I

grabbed it and dropped to my knees, gagging. The contents of my last meal spewed into the metal container. I bowed beside the can, hanging my head, breathing deeply. I managed to stumble to my feet and, for support, draped myself over a machine that hummed under my aching body. No one seemed fazed by the fact that I had just spent three minutes on my knees in agony. In fact, all four of the men grinned from ear to ear.

The shoe man stepped up to me and bowed. The captain said, "Radio officer."

I released my hold on the supportive equipment and flailed around for the waste bin. Kneeling and vomiting, I felt as if this would never end. Finally it did, and I rose to my feet. However, as soon as the third man was introduced, I fell to my knees again, retching. I clung tightly to the sides of the round receptacle, swaying on the floor with the rolling of the ship. My Cinderella slippers were long gone, having been lost in the first round of my wrestling match with the trash can.

Above me, I sensed no sympathy from my companions—only excited talking, interspersed with laughter. I retched so hard that my eyes watered and my stomach muscles cramped, doubling me over even further. I could not bear the misery of being so sick combined with the humiliation of puking in front of these strange, unconcerned men.

I staggered to my feet, now covered only in wool socks, trying to orient myself enough to get back down the stairway. One of the laughing men hurried forward and removed the reeking trash can. The captain handed me my boots, at the same time, motioning me down the stairs. I grasped the handrail at the top step and my knees buckled under me. On my butt, I bumped my way down the stairs and banged into the closed door at the bottom.

Somehow, I made it back to my cabin and dove onto the bottom bunk. A volcano out of control, my stomach churned and rolled, continuously threatening to erupt. My hands shook, and sweat drenched my clothes; hot flashes warred with the cold chills that shook me. A small trash can under my desk stood ready to take over duty from the one on the bridge. Thankfully, lying down helped, and I only had to reach for it once.

I tried to fluff up my hard pillow to make it more comfortable. It would not "fluff up." I poked at it feebly and tried to twist it into some sort of softer shape. It felt like a mound of hard sand encased in a scratchy cotton cloth, resisting my every jab. I wondered if all of the pillows on the boat matched the construction of this one. Perhaps this was a special observer pillow, meant to enhance my agony.

Everyone has her own method of coping with seasickness. I quickly learned that as long as I lay down completely flat, I would not throw up. The minute I sat up, however, I vomited. Finally identifying this as the way to manage my illness, I settled in to try to sleep it off. Then, of course, I had to answer the call at the other end of my body. Finding the toilet in the maze of the ship proved to be a formidable task. I lugged the trash can with me, stumbling around until I made myself understood. Twice I heaved into my trusty companion before finally making it to the toilet. Japanese eyes and laughter followed my every move. By this point, I no longer cared.

Indeed, as the skipper of the pilot boat had predicted, the weather kicked up again. The *Kyowa* rode like a roller coaster, pitching up and over mountainous waves as she headed out into the open sea. My cabin could have been mistaken for one of those paperweight winter-wonderland scenes—the kind you shake to make the snow fly. Notebooks, pens and pencils that I had foolishly laid out on my desk took to flight. My favorite tea mug smashed into the far wall and splintered into pieces. The drawer in the tiny desk slid open and crashed to the floor, skidding first into one corner, then another, a boxy ice skater gone mad. My wooden closet door banged open and shut, open and shut—thudding in time to the frenetic moves of the boat. I didn't have the strength to fasten things down. All I could do was brace myself in my bunk, fighting every roll and pitch of the ship and my ever-rising nausea. A far cry from my previous cruise in calm seas of the tropics . . . .

Every once in awhile, the cooking master waltzed in and waved various steaming, strange dishes under my nose, which only made things worse . . . a lot worse. Once he even lifted a piece of food from the plate, pushing it toward my lips and smacking his own. He turned and fled when I rose up like Frankenstein and lunged toward him. Of course, he assumed I was a madwoman, not realizing I was only after the trash can and not him. Later, he bravely crept again into my room, bringing me much-needed cans of juices and soft drinks.

I lost all track of time. Day and night ran together. My windowless cabin allowed no glimpse of the outside world. The digital watch I wore stayed set on Alaska time, but I had noticed the clock on the bridge read a totally different time, which I assumed was that of Japan. At first during this extended period of misery, I tried to track the time, needing desperately to stay oriented in this foreign world. Then I gave up; since death would probably take me any minute, it did not matter. I dozed fitfully, waking and peering through the darkness at the lighted display on my wrist. Sometimes minutes had passed, sometimes hours.

Thankfully my watch was equipped with a date display. Three days had gone by when I awoke from one of the endless dozes to realize that the boat was no longer being tossed about with wild abandon. In fact, we seemed to be rolling along in a constant forward motion.

I cautiously sat up in my bunk. My head spun as I slowly got out of bed. I stood up, grasping the upper bunk for support. Miracle of miracles—I didn't feel the onrush of nausea that had plagued me constantly for the past three days. Could it be? Was it really over? I took a few deep breaths, stretched my arms over my head and immediately smacked my hands into the ceiling. A few minutes passed, and I still felt no desire to throw myself on the floor and kneel over that wretched trash can.

I had won the first round, surviving the hell of seasickness. I recalled our class instructor telling us of observers who had been defeated by seasickness—some so violently ill from the minute they set foot on their boat that they had to radio NMFS (National

Marine Fisheries Service), giving up the job and requesting to return home. Early on, I had told myself that I would not be one of these. I needed to prove to myself—and to everyone else—that I was tough and that I could take it, whatever "it" was.

I remember my excitement at discovering the word feminist, sometime in junior high school—finally, a word that fit *me* as I struggled to define myself in my confining world. So what if my friends snickered at the mention of the word, or, worse yet, didn't know what it meant? I was relieved to have a name for the need I felt to prove myself equal to any man at any task set before me. Being a foreign fisheries observer required just about everything difficult—physical strength, stamina, endurance, living in harsh conditions and other things I didn't know yet. And, I felt at the time, these were the things that I had to conquer to prove myself as competent as any man in the program. They represented the *real* test.

I felt giddy, triumphant and tough, recalling that the instructor had used the masculine pronoun when he referred to the last observer who had returned home due to seasickness.

Wobbling to the door, I opened it, peering out into the corridor. There was no sign of life anywhere. Stiff and cramped, but feeling like I had been given a new lease on life, I decided to wander around and try to determine the lay of the ship. I slowly moved out of my cabin and headed left, grasping the handrail that lined the corridor walls for support. Three days of seasickness had robbed me of my strength, but it felt invigorating to simply be out of my sweaty bunk. Not only was my pillow filled with what surely had to be sand, but the mattress was stuffed with the same unyielding material. No feather beds on the *Kyowa*.

Suddenly, a door flew open and a young man stepped partially over a cabin threshold. He stopped abruptly when he saw me. Quickly he turned and said something over his shoulder. Instantly, four faces appeared behind him, peering around each other, trying to get a glimpse of me.

I smiled at the men and said, "*Ohayo Gozaimas.*"

This sent them off into gales of laughter. They jostled among themselves and, finally, the same fellow who "spoke English" and had shown me to the bridge stepped forward.

His face, once again, was bright red, and he grinned from ear to ear. He pointed to his nose and said, "Kazukisan."

"Oh, your name is Kazukisan" I smiled happily. "My name is Dail."

Kazukisan gazed at me blankly. I pointed to my nose, just as he had done, and said slowly "Dail."

Kazuki turned to confer with his friends. Someone found a piece of paper and pencil and Kazuki thrust these at me. I wrote my name out in capital letters. Taking the paper, Kazuki slowly read aloud my name—or his rendition of my name. It sounded close, but the "L" was giving him trouble. I remembered a friend's story of the Japanese diplomat who, at a political function in D.C., asked a campaigning Senator how his erection was going.

I repeated my name slowly. Kazuki's brow wrinkled in concentration. He conferred again with his friends. A couple of them grabbed the paper and scribbled on it. Eventually he turned back to me and said slowly, "Day-ru. Day-ru-san. "

And so I became Dairusan, the first American woman observer the *Kyowa Maru* had ever had on board. Only with my training class had the program begun placing women on Japanese ships. For years, their fishing companies and government had refused to have us on their vessels, feeling that this was an "unacceptable environment." Many fishermen also considered it bad luck to have women at sea. But if they wished to continue fishing in United States waters, they had to accept female observers. Alaskan waters provide exceptionally lucrative fishing grounds for the Japanese, producing millions of dollars worth of fish, so they acquiesced without much of a struggle.

I was very aware of the traditional view that Japanese men held of women. I was also very aware of the need to be respectful of a culture vastly different from my own. I have never felt the ethnocentricity that seems to afflict so many Americans; I wanted to try to "fit in" culturally. I needed to bury my own judgments and biases to do this "right"; to open my mind to a totally different way of viewing the world. Yet, at the same time, I was driven to show these men that I was tough, strong and capable. I refused to be viewed as a weak female. The characteristics that Japanese men valued in women were anathema to me: submissiveness, weakness, and servility. My mission, an easy one, was to portray none of these characteristics. I hoped I would not offend anyone by simply being myself.

FOUR

Table Manners

"Dairusan! Dairusan!"

A rapid knock on my door, and before I could reply, the smiling face of the cooking master peered into my room. He motioned for me to follow him. Since I was actually beginning to feel hungry, I fell into step with him.

"What is your name?" I asked slowly. He smiled in reply but said nothing. I pointed to my nose and said, "Dairusan," then pointed at him.

"Ahh!" His index finger paused just before his nose and said "Sasakisan." By now, I realized that instead of pointing to their chest, as we would, when referring to themselves, the men pointed to their noses.

"OK—Sasakisan." I returned his grin. Shining brown eyes and a salt-and-pepper crew-cut set off Sasakisan's constant smile. I guessed him to be in his fifties. He was a short, trim man with very large hands. His tight white T-shirt outlined a powerful, compact body.

Sasakisan led me into the tiny dining room, which was forward of the ship, near the bow. Three rows of wooden tables and benches packed the space running port to starboard. They were fixed to the floor and the walls. The ever-present fluorescent lighting glowed over the plastic flowered table covers and the sickly green walls. Huge Sumo wrestlers rolled around on the screen of a small Sony television mounted in one corner. Through a serving window at the rear of the room was the tiny kitchen where Sasakisan, alone, did all the cooking. Instead of the diesel-like smell from the corridor, the heavy air hung with the smells of grease and cigarette smoke.

Men packed the galley, and their response to my entrance varied. Several jumped to their feet and fled the room. Others giggled and poked each other. Two stood and motioned for me to sit down. I sat between these two men, one of whom I vaguely remembered as the captain from our initial meeting on the bridge. The captain's sweetly rounded face radiated kindness. He was a chubby fellow, and his soulful brown eyes glistened with intelligence and curiosity. He was so soft-spoken and gentle, I had trouble picturing him wearing the mantle of captain.

He gestured to the man across from me and said, "Fishing master." The two stood in direct contrast. Instead of somber and soulful eyes, the fishing master's danced with mischief. Even his wire-rimmed glasses couldn't hide their sparkle. Laugh lines creased an otherwise baby-smooth complexion. I pegged him at 45 or so. Later I would find my estimate had been 15 years too young. I envisioned him dressed in a red suit and white beard, a jolly Santa Claus.

Even with only 26 crew members, hierarchy ruled the galley seating arrangement. The captain explained that only officers sat at the "head" table. My officer status dictated that I sit with him, the fishing master, chief mate, and radio officer.

Sasakisan raced in with steaming plates of food, which he placed in front of the captain, fishing master and me. My round plastic plate contained a damp mound of unidentifiable slender stalks and two pieces of raw fish. I contemplated these items, wondering if my newly regained appetite would fade away. Sasakisan fairly skipped to a large pot on one end of the table and dished out three bowls of rice. Next he dashed back into the kitchen, returning with three bowls of a soup that contained bits of fish and potatoes. We were the only ones he waited on. All the other men crowded around the tiny galley window and served themselves.

All around me, men ate their soup with loud slurping sounds. The galley could have been a Hoover vacuum cleaner demonstration center. I watched the captain and fishing master hold their bowls up close to their mouths and, with artful chopstick manipulation, suck up their soup. Sasakisan brought my soup, and I ate it as most Americans do—quietly—a marked contrast to those around me. Later in the cruise, the men would encourage me to slurp while eating, clearly letting me know that this was the only way to truly enjoy food. They sat beside me, bowls raised, sucking air in preparation for the real thing, insisting that I follow their movements. I tried, but this was the one thing I could never bring myself to do in the entire eight weeks of eating meals with them. My Mama had done too good a job of ingraining table manners.

I tried to take my cues from the two officers with whom I was sitting. When they finished their soup, they began using their chopsticks to eat from their plates. Sasakisan had given me a knife and fork, but I wanted to learn how to eat with the real thing. I pointed to the captain's lacquered utensils and then at myself. He realized what I wanted and shouted something to Sasakisan, who came running with a pair of the shiny tools.

I was unsure even how to pick them up, though I had closely watched the captain and fishing master. I gripped the needle-like instruments tightly and went after a vegetable. Flipping from my fingers, one of the pointed missiles followed a trajectory path straight into the face of the fishing master. It bounced off of his glasses, and was followed by the soft thud of the vegetable, which slid from the glass lens down his cheek. Just as it reached his mouth, the fishing master stuck out his tongue and captured the runaway stalk. The table erupted into loud laughter which, thankfully, the fishing master joined.

After this fiasco, one of the men at the other end of the table moved to sit near me—and teach me chopstick etiquette. He introduced himself as Masadru. I instantly thought of a Kewpi doll. A slim face, surrounded by short, springy black hair sat atop his wiry frame. Later in the cruise, he would confess that he had given himself a permanent wave to obtain these locks. He refused to believe that my short red curls were natural and not aided by chemicals.

I imitated Masadru's eating technique as closely as I could, providing entertainment for everyone in the galley. Other fishermen decided to get into the act. Soon I was surrounded by an entire group, waving their miniature batons, proudly giving lessons to their novice twirler. Instead of cramps from seasickness, my stomach ached from continuous laughter.

After the decidedly hilarious meal, the captain motioned for me to follow him to the bridge.

"*Arigato*, Sasakisan!" Sasakisan's face lit up when I said thank you, and he bent forward slightly and smiled as I left. From class, I knew that one person bowed to another to show respect. Other crew members would often bow to me. Mindful of hierarchical etiquette, I did not return their offerings but always bowed to the officers, the only people on the ship who were my "superiors."

I had begun to identify subtle landmarks on the *Kyowa*. Masadru lived behind a door whose symbols were round and curly, like his hair. The character on Kazukisan's cabin contained three horizontal slashes. I strode behind the captain and easily recognized the door to the bridge, which had small red writing beneath the main black characters. Of course, the living area was only one small part of the boat—I had yet even to go out on deck or down into the fish factory.

We emerged from the dark stairway onto the bridge, and I blinked, trying to adjust to the daylight after so long under the artificial glow of fluorescence. I looked around at the equipment that had appeared so mysterious through my seasick haze. The captain pointed out various devices crowding the compact space. Some I knew, others would remain a mystery to me right up until I left the ship. I recognized the Loran unit, which showed a digital reading of the ship's latitude and longitude. The old-fashioned wooden steering wheel, surrounded by high-tech navigational equipment, stood prominently in front of the window facing forward. The fishing master cackled loudly at someone over the VHF radio, which hung by the chart table. Determined to make a show of strength on this visit to the bridge, I marched over to the charts spread out on the wooden surface. Using the reading from the Loran, I pinpointed our location: several hundred miles north of the Aleutian islands, in the middle of the Bering Sea. No surprises here. Leaning over the table, I swung my leg and kicked an object that tipped over. I bent down to see what I had disturbed, and my old companion, the metal trash can, rolled out and bumped against my shin. I hastily stuffed it back under the table, hoping this was not an omen.

The captain motioned me over to a waist high desk, on which he had spread out the ship's trawl logbooks. As the observer, I had unconditional access to these, the official records of the ship's catches, and would need to check them daily. I pretended to understand as his finger traced line after line of indistinguishable words, written in tiny Japanese script. The captain flipped the page. Nodding thoughtfully, I wrinkled my forehead. I like to think this is my intelligent look.

I wondered when we would begin fishing. I pulled out my Japanese/English dictionary and questioned the captain. Finally understanding my query, he looked up the word "tomorrow" and underlined it carefully with a pencil. My stomach knotted with anxiety. So many pieces of the puzzle of my work remained a mystery. I did not even know where the factory was, had no idea what the processing equipment looked like, barely knew my way to the deck . . . and setting up my work station was a mammoth task in itself. My mind reeled with the things I had to do before the first net was brought aboard.

My watch said that it was 2 p.m. As I remembered, the clock on the bridge read something totally different. For the entire voyage, I would remain thoroughly confused by the time differences between the ship, my watch (Alaska time) and Greenwich Mean Time (GMT), which I was required to use in my work.

I looked up the word "tour" and showed it to the captain. He nodded vigorously and made an announcement over the loudspeaker.

"Kazukisan come here soon. He is your assistant to help you. Help English, help work. OK?" The captain surprised me with his English.

Within minutes, Kazukisan appeared. When he saw me, he blushed violently. Kazukisan, I had decided, was a very earnest young man and eager to please. His round face was sweetly cherubic. He and the captain talked for a few minutes, and he started off down the stairs, looking over his shoulder for me to follow.

I stopped by my cabin to gather my warm clothing. Wool sweater, polypropylene jacket and raingear. The living area of the ship was fairly warm, but I knew it would be bitterly cold outside. I grabbed my steel-toed boots to put on just before stepping onto the deck. After my disastrous faux pas on the bridge, I wore only Birkenstocks in the living quarters of the ship and kept my boots on standby behind my cabin door.

I followed Kazukisan to the tightly bolted door that led to the deck, the same one I had come through on my first day on the ship. In the small changing room beside the door, Kazukisan yanked down a pair of black rubberized coveralls from the dozens hanging on hooks. While he donned his coveralls, I put my rain gear on over my warm clothes. I loved the cheerful yellow color of my shiny new gear. The shade would last about four days before the fish slime took over, turning my sunny outfit a sickly green.

My companion's gear seemed meant for a person several sizes larger than me. He hoisted his pants almost up to his chest and pulled a beige strap, like a rubber band, around them so they wouldn't slide off. The cuffs of his jacket had been rolled up several times but still his gloved fingers barely peeked out from the ends. We grinned at each other, two sausages encased in plastic, ready for the display case.

Kazukisan pulled open the hatchway. I stepped out onto the deck and immediately spun sideways into the port railing, buffeted by the force of the wind. I clung to the icy railing, struggling to remain upright, averting my face from the burning gale. I inched along behind Kazukisan, the railing my lifeline. The searing wind threatened to blow my contact lenses right out of my eyes. Slowly we made our way over the icy deck to the stern of the boat, leaning into the fierce wind as we plodded forward. We circumnavigated

coils of nets, lines and other fishing gear in piles that towered over
me, menacing with their unsteady wobbling. What if I got crushed
by one of these before I even made it to the factory? Would I be
given a burial at sea? Or perhaps I would be stuffed into the fish
freezer, laid out beside frozen blocks of pollock, until the *Kyowa*
returned with my body to Dutch Harbor.

Before I could further develop these thoughts, we reached the
stern. Kazukisan opened a hatchway and led me down into the
fish processing area. I closed my eyes and sniffed, my mind filled
with olfactory images of coastal North Carolina seafood shops, a
briny low tide smell mingling with the scent of freshly caught
creatures; but overlying it all, the odor from day old fish, edging
close to rotten, piled out on the dock behind the shop.

After I spent countless hours in this environment, the factory
air would become just another part of me, rather like the hair on
my head or, say, my left leg. My nose would no longer twinge at
the pungent aroma surrounding me. (In fact, when my cruise was
completed, I ended up flying back to Seattle wearing my rain jacket.
Though I had cleaned it as best I could, my friends who picked
me up at the airport refused to allow me into their house with the
jacket on. I had wondered why no one sat beside me on the flight
home . . . .)

A gleaming, wet maze, the processing area stretched before me
like a football field, an entire world under the deck. White pipes of
all sizes snaked haphazardly along the low ceiling, a plumber's
nightmare. Behind me, flush against the stern of the vessel, loomed
two cavernous fish bins, immobile Dempsey Dumpsters built into
the ship. Metal chutes and endless conveyor belts that moved the
fish along the processing line packed every inch of the factory floor.
The equipment glistened in the dull fluorescent glow from the
overhead lights. We had studied factory diagrams in training class,
but I anxiously wondered if I would ever be able to figure out this
chute and ladder puzzle that confronted me. I envisioned thousands
of fish flying along the conveyor belts, too fast for me to keep up,
as I trotted alongside, trying to grab the slimy creatures.

The only elemental difference between the deck and factory

was the absence of the howling wind. I puffed out air, watching my breath hover, cloud-like, before me. How would I manage to stay even semi-comfortable for hours on end down here? I stamped my numb feet in a futile effort to keep them warm. Already blocks of ice, they seemed more of a hindrance than a help as I stumbled along behind Kazukisan, trying to keep up.

To do my job, I needed to set up a work station near the beginning of the processing line. There I would remove samples of the catch for weighing and measuring. I spotted an area that seemed appropriate, and motioning to Kazukisan, indicated that I would work here. He nodded vigorously and said, "I tell Akihamasan you here work." I vaguely remembered a man named Akihama being introduced to me as the factory master.

Kazukisan helped me haul my baskets, scales and other work equipment to the spot I had chosen. We hung the scales from one of several sturdy overhead pipes. Kazuki found tools and we constructed a wooden work bench. As we worked, we stamped our feet and clapped various body parts, trying to keep the blood flowing. When we had built the waist-high bench, I asked Kazuki to help me measure the fish holding bins. One of my tasks would be to estimate total catch size, and one way of doing this was by a volume (how much the fish bins held) and density (dependent upon the type of catch) formula. These bins appeared to be fairly easy to measure, so this seemed the most efficient way of calculating catch size. Kazukisan raised a wooden door that allowed fish to flow out of the bin and onto the first conveyor belt.

I climbed onto the belt, dragging plastic forms with me, and squeezed through the narrow door way into the fish bins, Kazukisan close behind. I stood up inside the box-like cave and immediately slipped on the wet metal floor, sliding with the rolling of the ship until I stopped against the starboard wall of the bin. My plastic forms fell to the floor and slid into the corner with the next pitch of the ship. Kazukisan nose-dived after the thin sheets and, staggering to his feet, clutched them against his rubberized chest. Daylight from an opening above my head trickled feebly over us. I fumbled in my jacket pocket for the heavy, waterproof tape measure and flicked the release button. The sharp-edged metal tape sprung out of the holder like a coiled snake, stopping its slithering motion only when it hit one of foundation posts in the middle of the bin. I forced the out-of-control snake into every corner and crevice of the dark prison, stretching and pulling and calling out numbers to Kazukisan, who dutifully recorded them with a slime proof pencil on the plastic forms.

Measurements completed, we crawled back out the doorway and into the factory. I asked Kazukisan to describe the flow of the fish and processing to me. He led off on another brisk jog around the factory, dodging sharp edges and dangerous-looking machinery, pausing to point and exclaim. As with the captain's trawl log book explanation, I nodded, looking thoughtful, comprehending nothing of what he said. I did not worry about my total lack of understanding. By tomorrow, assuming the captain's estimates were accurate, I would be in the middle of processing a trawl and all would become clear. Or so I naively believed.

FIVE

Fishing

EARLY NEXT MORNING, I AWOKE TO A STRANGE, UNIDENTIFIABLE sensation. Then I got it: Generally the ship's engines hummed continuously and the vessel itself vibrated and throbbed from their power. Now, however, there was no roar of engines or forward, pulsing movement—the boat rolled gently from side to side. I threw on my clothes and raced to the bridge, worried we might already be trailing a net behind us.

I was greeted by the captain and the fishing master, who told me, "Soon fishing begin." I hunched over the electronic fish finder alongside the fishing master.

"*Mintai. Mintai.*" He repeated as he tapped the glass surface of the fish finder, his finger hovering over a deep red blob. *Mintai,* or pollock, school densely in large numbers, which explained the intense red display on the fish finder screen.

I stared, fascinated, at the patterns on the fish finder. Jagged black lines arched up from the bottom of the screen, tall pyramids of underwater cliffs. The *mintai* pattern appeared wedged between two peaks, just below the pointed tops. I wondered how they could possibly draw a net through this narrow opening. Two yellow patches streaked like brush strokes across the far left of the screen. I tapped these stripes, and the fishing master spoke a name that I did not recognize.

I moved to the stern window and gazed down on the deck. Below me, the entire crew moved carefully and quickly in a finely choreographed routine. Coils of rope winged across the deck, tossed from one man to another, props in their energetic ballet. They wasted no movement as they readied the deck. Four men danced with large cables attached to winches, muscling their recalcitrant partners across the deck, where they clipped the hooked cables to the main fishing net, heaped in one corner. Slowly the mesh net lifted into the air, swaying and shivering, a huge caterpillar awakening, section by section.

The fishing master stood beside me, concentrating on the scene below. He shouted into a microphone, directing the positioning of the net. Finally, he barked a clipped command. Several men slid the heavily weighted end of the net down the ramp, where it splashed into the sea. With a whine, the winches began unwinding the heavy lengths of cable attached to the net, and the boat moved slowly forward, trailing the net out behind it. The weights strung at regular intervals along the bottom sides of the net forced it downward.

When the crew finished laying the net, the massive trawl doors followed. They hung like giant shields, affixed to posts on each side of the stern ramp. Once in the water, these two 1.5 ton metal door-shaped objects kept the mouth of the net spread open as it moved through the school of fish. The fishing master shouted a command, and four men stepped up to the steel plates, wrestling them from their perch. A terrible grinding and clanging crackled onto the bridge over the loudspeaker, like special effects at a Halloween haunted house. The captain, bent over a depth sounder, shouted numbers to the fishing master, whose gaze never wavered from the deck. After several minutes, he raised the microphone to his lips and commanded the crew to stop the net. More grinding and then sudden silence. The soft clicking and humming of the bridge instruments crept into the quiet.

Like its smell, the sounds of the *Kyowa* would become part of my psyche. I had never been in a situation where I could not rely on verbal communication for my direction. How could I gain the information I needed to do my job? I found my clues in the sounds and feel of the boat. My senses stayed on heightened awareness, a constant adrenalin rush that exhausted me. From a deep sleep, I would claw my way to consciousness, wondering why, then realize that we were stopped dead in the water, rolling gently, the absence of engine sounds creating a vacuum of silence. I knew the crew would be on deck, preparing to set the net. The whine of the winches brought me running to the bridge; a net was going out. A slow pitching and soft humming guaranteed that I would find the fishing master huddled over the fish finder, studying it intently as we slowly moved through the ocean, searching for fish.

I wondered how long the trawl would stay down. Minutes? Hours? The school of fish on the fish finder screen appeared very dense—did that mean the net would fill up quickly? And just how much fish could that net hold anyway? I pointed to my watch and looked questioningly at the fishing master. He held up two fingers and shrugged, which I interpreted to mean two hours.

I started to pace back and forth in front of the window. Despite my determination to prove to myself and everyone else that I could do this work, niggling doubts taunted me. Maybe I really *couldn't* do it. Would I physically be able to weigh and measure enough fish to provide accurate samples? Would the statistical calculations be too difficult? What if all of the data I brought back to land was inaccurate, weeks of work wasted? Not only did I have to prove myself, but my work played a major part in the role of the U.S. government's management of the Bering Sea fisheries. I envisioned returning to land, having failed at my job. Facing the program staff and trying to explain how I had managed to ruin everything: inaccurate samples, not enough samples, mis-identified fish . . . How would I feel? How would I be viewed by the program? I thought about the days leading up to this point, where the real work began. The terrifying scramble to get to the deck of the *Kyowa*—staring down into those hungry waves, knowing what would happen with just one misstep. Rolling around in my bunk for three days, turned inside out from seasickness. Somehow I would pull this off; I had come too far not to. I went down to my sampling station and nervously shoved baskets around for a few minutes—arranged, for the fifth time, my plastic forms on the wooden work bench—and headed to the galley for sustenance before I faced whatever lay ahead.

Within 90 minutes, bells began ringing, and I recognized the characteristic whine of the winches. My battle plan, reviewed over and over, took me first to the bridge to watch as the trawl came on. Then I would race to the changing room and don my gear. Finally, I would appear in position, at attention beside my work station, ready to attack the fish as they came into the factory.

From the bridge window, I watched in awe as the crew, with great difficulty, winched an enormous net jammed full of fish onto the deck. The monstrous net appeared to be alive, writhing like a huge whale that bucked and fought against every effort to land it on board. Water poured over the deck as the packed net swung crazily through the air, threatening to steamroll everything in its way. Crew members leapt and twisted to avoid this unpredictable enemy. When the thing finally lay still on the deck, it stretched from end to end, about 125 feet long and 12 feet tall, towering over the men beside it.

Beside me, the fishing master and the captain exclaimed excitedly. I felt hot all over; the roll bar, gripped tightly under my hands, became slippery with sweat. I had imagined many scenarios, but none like this. In my mental preparations, we pulled on a trawl of, perhaps, 10-20 tons. Something that would fill up the two 5-ton holding bins twice. The sheer quantity of fish that wallowed below on the deck was beyond my comprehension. What was I going to do? What would any of us do?

Wiping my damp hands on my coveralls, I caught the attention of the fishing master and wrote "50?" on a piece of paper. He laughed and wrote "90!" Ninety tons of fish . . . Lord have mercy.

The deck below remained a stage, the men jerking like marionettes. They bounced from one end to the other, dragging dangling cables like puppet strings. Shaking loose their ties, they attached the lines to various parts of the net. The puppet masters took over, operating the winches, lifting the mammoth sausage up, up into the air. Section by section, they emptied the net into the holding bins. Like silver dollars, the fish flashed as they slid in mountainous heaps into the bins.

I went below to put on my gear and figure out what I was

going to do. I arrived to pure chaos in the processing factory below the deck. Fish poured out of the holding bins, spilling wildly off the conveyor belts. Men scurried around attempting to pile up the fish, which stubbornly insisted on slithering about on the floor like oversized threatening bananas. Some crewmen turned on the mechanized saws, others hand sharpened fillet knives. Akihamasan, the factory master, shouted orders. Slowly, fish began moving along the conveyor belt. The factory became its own sea of fish and noise—the high keening of the saws, the grinding of the conveyor belts, the shouting of the men. Very different from the quiet area that Kazukisan and I had visited the day before. I stuffed in my earplugs to try to drown out the overwhelming clatter.

Kazukisan, assigned to be my "assistant," appeared at my side, a dazed look on his face. "Too many fishes!" he exclaimed. I could only agree. He gazed at me expectantly, and I realized he was waiting for directions from me. I tried to look like I knew what I was doing and motioned for him to help me slide my sampling baskets next to the conveyor belt. We had been taught to take the entire contents of one section of the belt for a sample. I bent over the conveyor belt and, using my hands and arms, slid as much fish as I could in the general direction of the baskets. Most of the fish flopped to the floor behind the baskets and proceeded to disappear from view beneath the conveyor belt. I tried to repeat the process, but by this time the fish were moving at such a rapid clip along the belt that I succeeded in swiping only a few into the baskets. I had little to show for my two attempts at sample collection, other than a nice coating of fish slime on my yellow rain jacket. Some of the slime worked its way under the neckline of my wool sweater, and I wriggled as it oozed down my chest. I glanced at Kazuki, who looked as if he were trying not to laugh.

Leaning close to him, I shouted, "Please, can you have Akihamasan turn off the conveyor belt for just two minutes?"

He smiled at me and nodded eagerly but did not move. I went into my pantomime routine, indicating that the belt should be stopped, I would quickly fill my baskets with fish, then the belt could be started again. This time as he nodded, Kazuki raced off to find Akihama. When they returned, it took five more minutes of pantomime for Akihamasan to understand what I needed. Finally, he ordered the conveyor shut off and Kazuki and I filled my six sampling baskets.

We shoved each basket over to my work station, and I slowly sorted the fish into various species groups. The previous night I had dreamed of bringing on a rummage sale of fish, dozens of different species jumbled together, all sizes and shapes and none that I could identify. I had tried to sort them into piles, but they had been hopelessly tangled, like a huge knotted silver necklace. I was relieved to see that this trawl proved what they had told me in class: Pollock catches are relatively "clean" ones with little by-catch. Pollock made up most of my sample. A few pacific cod leered out at me, and a king crab anxiously flailed its pinchers.

Kazuki and I heaved each basket up and, using the rope and clip especially designed for this purpose, attached it to my hanging scales. Steadying the basket, I tried to get as accurate a reading as possible, despite the rolling of the ship. I recorded the weights on my plastic forms. Later, I would use a statistical calculation to extrapolate the sample sizes up to estimate how much of each species was contained in the entire catch. I also had to collect weight and length statistics for all king crab, halibut and salmon. Luckily, the crewmen were experienced in the ways of observers, and they pulled the few of these contained in the trawl off of the line for me and set them aside. Even if these prohibited species were dead, I had to toss them over. Though this often seemed a waste, the trainers explained it this way: Suppose, for instance, the captain pointed out a freezer full of halibut and said they had all been dead when they came on as by-catch in an earlier trawl. Before my arrival, the boat could have set a net specifically for halibut and now claim simply that they had not wanted to waste this "accidental" catch. So United States law stated that it was illegal for foreign boats to have these species on board in any form.

After finishing my third stint of sampling, I jumped onto the processing line beside Masadru. His curls flew back and forth as he turned from side to side, shoving fish from one conveyor to another. I pantomimed that I wanted to help, and he shouted to Kazuki, who handed me a knife. Kazuki positioned me in front of my very own chopping block, and I watched as he demonstrated how to chop the tails off of the fish. I grabbed a foot-long pollock and placed it on the block. Whacking at its tail, I only partially severed it. I picked up the fish and shook it vigorously to see if I could dislodge the tail. No luck. Kazuki poked the man beside him, who alerted other crew members to the spectacle. Even over the clattering factory sounds, I could hear their laughter. I kept at it and eventually got the whacking motion down. Of course, the men around me cut off six tails for every one I managed to remove.

Before returning to my sampling work, I walked through the factory, trying to understand the work flow. I passed the "linemen," whom I had attempted to assist with my tail-whacking efforts. They headed, gutted and tailed each fish. The last lineman shoved the dressed fish onto a conveyor belt that spewed them onto a table where they piled up in front of three men. These men hunted through the piles of fish, picking and choosing ones to wedge against each other in large metal pans, a jigsaw puzzle of pollock. Once the puzzle was completed, the men sprayed the pans with water and placed them on freezer racks in the flash freezer behind them. The fish stayed here for several hours, until they became solid blocks of ice. Then a crew member removed the frozen blocks of fish and another man placed these blocks in cartons. Each block weighed 25 kilograms and each carton contained two blocks. The packed cartons received a date stamp and the word *mintai* in Japanese characters. Then came the final ride for these fish, as they careened on the angled conveyor down to the depths of the frozen fish holds below. I jumped onto the conveyor and rode on top of two cartons, past the astonished faces of the packers, to the dark opening of the fish hold. The boxes burst through the tiny doorway into two black-gloved hands. I perched on the sill above the doorway, peering into the dimness, trying to see through the icy steam. The hands belonged to a man yanking cartons off the conveyor. A heavy wool hat pulled low over his face obscured his identity. He and a second anonymous man waddled like bears in their bundled clothing, stacking the cardboard boxes against the wall.

I returned to the processing line, where the crew members worked fast and furiously, slicing and sawing. Fish guts and body parts flew, covering everything. My shiny yellow rain suit became slimy and brownish-green, as did my boots, gloves and hard hat. I had learned the hard way that I must wear the protective yellow plastic hat in the factory; on my earlier tour with Kazuki, I had banged my head three times on the low hanging pipes.

Using sea-water hoses, we washed things down, including ourselves, sluicing offal (fish waste) and debris out the metal chutes at water level into the sea. I repeated my sampling procedure every few hours, at various points during the processing, in an attempt to get unbiased samples of the catch. Despite the overwhelming number of fish, my work was not technically too difficult—it just stretched over long periods of time.

After my second sampling stint, Kazuki had returned to the processing line, leaving me to work alone. Now, each time I hoisted the heavy baskets (about 75 pounds when full) onto the hanging scales for weighing, men would shout and prod each other to watch me. Sometimes the flashing knives would come to a standstill as they gaped, open mouthed in amazement, at this Amazon *gaijen ona* (foreign woman).

After nine hours or so, the bells sounded. The men turned off the clattering saws and someone stopped the conveyors. Sudden silence filled the factory. Akihamasan shouted an order, and the crew members raced topside to the deck. I followed the men and watched them set the net for another trawl.

This trawl remained in the water for only an hour, and I went up to the bridge to watch a repeat of what had occurred only 10 hours ago. To make way for this new catch, the crew pushed the remaining fish from the first trawl—a good 25 tons—to the sides of the boat. The men struggled to bring on another net packed with fish. It appeared to be about the same size as the first one—another 90 tons. I was incredulous—where would they put it? We still had over half the first trawl left to process. Once the net was landed, it looked like a football field of fish. The men clambered over piles of fish, slipping and sliding their way back down to the factory. I thought longingly of my sand-filled mattress and pillow, thinking how good they would feel right now. But instead of veering for my cabin, I forced myself to return to the factory.

After 12 hours in the factory, we took a quick break in the evening for a meal. The traditional meals of breakfast, lunch and dinner would not apply when we worked long stints in the factory. The hours blurred together and meals could no longer be identified by the time at which they were served. I was learning about the Japanese work ethic—hard work and lots of it. On larger boats, there were two shifts of crew members. However, on the *Kwoya*, the 26 crewmen worked constantly around the clock until the hauls were completed. The captain and even the cooking master joined us in the factory to try to cope with all of the fish. Never once did the fishing master come to the factory; I learned that, on Japanese boats, the fishing master outranks the captain and it would be unheard of for him to appear in the factory.

I worked until I was so exhausted that I tripped over my baskets and landed head first in a heap of pollock. It was around 2 a.m. when I left the factory. I stumbled to the changing room, where I would leave my rain gear. Slowly I struggled to straighten each arm as I removed my jacket. I sat heavily down on the floor, leaning over to reach my boots. My fingers were so weak that I could barely grasp them. I pulled and tugged, my arms and hands trembling with exhaustion. It seemed an impossible task to separate my boots from my feet. These were only my first two trawls—how could I keep this pace up for weeks at a time?

I returned to the factory at nine the next morning, my body protesting at every step. The men were still hard at work, with piles of fish remaining on the deck. They looked tired, but most still maintained their good humor. Akihamasan, the factory manager, gave me a weary smile of greeting. About my height, he stood out from the rest of the men. Despite the long hours in the factory, his agile hands still flew through the piles of fish. I questioned him about rest, and he told me when this haul was finished, the crew would sleep for a few hours before setting the net and beginning the whole process again. They had stopped for a meal break at some point while I was sleeping.

I bent over to shove my sampling baskets up to the conveyor belt and nearly fell over. But it was worse when I tried to straighten up again. I had to grab my work station for support and, literally, pull myself upright. I glanced around, hoping none of the men noticed.

Eventually, the conveyor belt from the holding bin carried only two or three pollock per foot, instead of a mass of fish wedged end to end. A couple of men climbed into the bins and shoveled the remaining fish out into the factory. The piles diminished. The whirring saws were shut down, knives cleaned and put away. My shoulders sagged and my boots pulled like steel weights. I felt beaten down by fish. Looking around at the exhausted men, I wondered how they still managed to stand upright.

After cleaning up, we all plodded towards the galley. Sasakisan had prepared a feast for us: steaming vats of rice plus lots of fried pollock and cabbage. Kazukisan and Akihamasan made room for me, and I wearily slumped between them. The men attacked the food as if they had not eaten in weeks. A bottle of whiskey made its rounds, then another and another. Sasakisan distributed cans of cold Kirin beer to the crew. Despite their exhaustion, the men laughed and chattered with an energy I did not feel. Akihamasan shyly offered me first beer, then whiskey. I could tell by his hesitancy that it was probably unusual for a woman to drink alcohol. Since I was *gaijin* and a guest, I am sure he felt compelled to offer it to me. The men all looked my way to see what I would do when Akihama plunked the whiskey bottle down in front of me. A couple of them whispered to each other. Masadru actually stood up from his seat at the end of the bench to get a better view. I could almost see their thoughts, hanging in the air like cartoon bubbles: Of course, this bizarre foreigner would certainly grab the bottle and chug down its entire contents. After all, for a woman who tossed around heavy baskets of fish and rode on conveyor belts, a bottle of whiskey would be child's play.

I felt like I was back in fifth grade being dared by the boys to climb out onto that wavering limb—come on, do it, don't be chicken! I find it difficult to pass up a dare. In this case, however, my palate won out. I abhor the taste of alcohol, so I asked Sasakisan for Coca-cola. Laughter and sighs of relief from the men. At least in one respect I did not blow their cultural expectations. Maybe this *gaijin ona* wasn't so different from the women they knew after all.

Being in the galley this time with the men was very different from our first meal together. It was as if I had proved myself by working side by side with them through the endless hours and piles of fish. Most of the men now acknowledged me, and only a few continued to avoid me. It seemed we were warming up to each other. However, even after two months of working together, a certain distance would remain. After I left the *Kyowa*, I worked on other Japanese vessels and had the same experience. We never attained an easy level of casualness, the give and take that comes from being together 24 hours a day. There always seemed to be an invisible barrier separating us; no matter what I did, I was never able to cross it. I attributed this to cultural differences and to the most significant difference of all—that I was a woman. I knew the importance of formality and politeness in Japanese culture. The attributes of reserve and respect when dealing with others are highly valued. I am not a reserved person; I am a person who laughs, teases and touches others with ease. I treaded a delicate balance everyday on the *Kyowa* and all of my other Japanese boats.

After eating, the weary men headed off to the showers and then to their bunks. I waited until all of the men finished bathing before I took my turn. I had been given a cardboard sign to post on the door that said "Off Limits" in Japanese. Or so the captain told me—I guessed that it probably said "Woman in shower—come on in!" I peeked hesitantly into the bathing room, hoping I would not see any naked men. Fortunately, it was empty. Hot steam filled the room, and dampness swam over me, even as I stood in the corridor. I hung my warning sign on the door knob, kicked off my sandals and stepped into the steam bath. Beneath my bare feet, damp wooden floorboards actually felt spongy after standing for long hours on the steel floor of the factory. A round tub full of hot salt water took up most of the space in the small square room. I groped along the wall until I found hooks on which to hang my towel and clothes.

Just as I stepped into the tub, the ship rolled to starboard. I gripped the sides of the tub for balance, my left foot skidding along the floor board, my right leg caught over the edge of the tub. I could have been on a football field, leading the cheerleading team in an acrobatic split. My clothes leapt from their hook and landed in a heap beside my left foot. The ship rolled to port and my split changed angle, pulling the other half of my groin muscles to match. Water sloshed over the tub's edge onto my clothing, flattening it into a soggy pile against the floorboards. Finally we leveled out, and I raised my aching left leg into the tub, sinking slowly up to my neck in the warm, relaxing water. I glanced down, once, at my clothes absorbing water on the floor but could not muster the strength to get out and hang them up. Instead, I rested my head back against the edge of the tub and drifted into a dreamy trance as the water flowed around me.

I must have dozed, because I dreamed of hundreds of pollock, swimming around me in the tiny tub, stacked up by the dozens in the room, hanging by their gills from the clothing hooks. My head snapped up; I looked around for fish. I forced myself to climb out of the tub and lather my body and hair. Bathing etiquette dictated that no soap get in the hot tub; it was to be kept as clean as possible. A shower head protruded from the starboard wall, and I turned the handle. I forced myself to stand under a freezing spray of salt water to rinse off. There was no fresh water in the shower. I would eventually become used to the salty crust that coated my body for the entire cruise. My hair, however, was another story. It always dried into stiff spikes that sprang straight out from my head, refusing to be flattened by my harsh brushing. Styled into punk before anyone knew what the word meant.

Shivering, I tried to dry off with my wet towel. I struggled to pull on blue jeans now heavy with water. I stepped into the corridor and thrust on my sandals, tiptoeing wetly back to my cabin, my dripping towel trailing behind me.

Throwing off my soaking clothes, I sank gratefully into my tiny bunk. Even my hard, sand-packed mattress felt welcoming in my exhausted state. I longed to stretch all the way out—an impossibility. I wondered how taller observers managed. The best I could do was a semi-fetal position, quickly falling asleep to the rhythm of the boat's gentle pitching.

SIX

Secret Codes

PAPERWORK! THE BANE OF AN OBSERVER'S EXISTENCE. DAILY MY EYES crossed over the 11 different and very detailed data forms that I filled out by hand, with my special number two pencil clutched tightly between my fingers. For each trawl I sampled, the forms had to be filled out, and I also had to write up daily and weekly catch reports.

When I finished my work in the factory, I would hose off the plastic field forms and length frequency strips on which I had recorded all of my raw data, and trudge back to my cabin. Cold salt water from the awkward, three-foot-long length frequency strips inevitably drained down my sleeves. No matter how carefully I rinsed, fish slime and other particles of factory debris clung to the forms. The slime would smear the metal surface of my tiny desk and coat parts of the paper data forms, as well.

I spent hours under the weak fluorescent lighting in my cabin, hunched over papers with tiny boxes. From my plastic forms, I transferred the weight and length figures for each species to one paper form. Next I used another form and my handheld calculator to do complex statistical calculations. I repeated each calculation at least twice to check for accuracy. Sometimes when the ship rolled sharply, I punched an incorrect button—say subtract instead of add. A slight problem. Once assured I had done my calculations correctly, I wrote the final figures onto yet another data sheet.

Finally, the only remaining task lay stretched before me—the yard-long, slimy, length frequency strip. These contained single straight-line tally marks, penciled in against the nose of each individual pollock. Painstakingly, I scratched each of more than one hundred marks onto the final paper forms, under the correct measurement heading. No matter how I tried to line everything up, halfway through my careful marking, I would often discover that I had my ruler off by one or two inches. Back, literally, to square one.

I would often review my completed data forms, which I kept in a big black notebook. By the legibility of my handwriting, I could reconstruct what the seas had been like. Clear, crisp numbers meant calm seas; jerky, smeared writing meant I had probably been bracing myself against the wall to write with the heavy rolling of the ship.

I also had to compare my catch estimates and species content findings with the captain's recordings, which he kept in a Daily Cumulative Catch Log (DCCL) on the bridge. Theoretically, my data figures should come close to the captain's DCCL figures. If not, a problem existed somewhere. The bottom line was that the boats wanted to catch as much fish as possible, with as little interference as possible. Each boat worked on a quota system, and once their quotas were up—based on my figures, monitored back on land—they had to stop fishing.

And what was an observer to do if some sort of problem existed on board? What if I suspected my boat of inaccurately reporting its catch sizes? Of secretly stashing prohibited species? Of any violation? We as observers did not have legal powers; the National Marine Fisheries Service, who directed the program back in Seattle, advised us to contact them for help. The only NMFS program contact available to us was through the ship's radio operator. Each week, we were required to send in a catch report via this radio operator. The report contained the names and amounts of each species that had been caught for the week. For instance, one of my reports might read:

Pollock 120,000 MT stop Pacific Cod 400 MT stop
Sculpin 4 MT stop Halibut 7 stop King Crab 14 stop
Fishing area 60° 15' North 178° 37' West stop March 13-19

These reports were standardized and the only variances were the names of the species caught and their amounts. To ensure that they had been received exactly as we sent them, part of our job on return to land was to verify their accuracy. Ships' operators had, on occasion, been known to alter numbers.

Before heading off to sea, NMFS had given each of us "secret codes" that we were to insert in our weekly radio messages if we perceived a problem. There were four escalating levels of codes, and to ensure secrecy, the program changed them with each observing group. Cleverly, these were disguised as names of fish that would normally never appear in our messages—species that we would never be catching in our particular areas. For example:

Level One: Herring—"I think there is a problem of cheating but am unsure. Will update with next radio message."

Level Two: Swordfish—"I am sure there is a problem of cheating but need more time to collect evidence. Will update with next radio message."

Level Three: Puffer fish—"I have documented cheating. Have Coast Guard board immediately."

Level Four: Angelfish—"My life is in danger. Have Coast Guard board immediately."

My training class had laughed at this last code. I think, however, our laughter was similar to that expressed during the survival suit drill—a cover for our very real nervousness. NMFS assured us that the foreigners stood to lose absolutely everything if they threatened an observer and this code had never been used.

Each of us, as green and trusting observers, took these codes to heart and with us to sea. We spent hours developing ingenious ways to hide the codes. My friend Joan used a laminating machine and made a small plastic square which she tucked beneath the insole of her boot. I inserted a thin card in the space between the paper and the cardboard tube of one of my extra rolls of toilet paper. Sara inked hers in tiny letters on the inside of her duffel bag.

I felt the confidence that comes with knowing I had a back up, an authority to turn to—help was only a radio message away. I wasn't *really* alone out here; if I found myself in a dangerous or threatening situation, all I had to do was send in the word "angelfish" and NMFS would immediately dispatch the Coast Guard to my rescue. This reassurance surrounded me like a protective bubble as, every day, I worked and socialized and laughed with the men, never forgetting I was an outsider in the midst of this foreign world.

One morning, the day after I submitted my weekly radio message to the ship's operator, the captain and fishing master summoned me to the bridge. I bounced cheerfully up to the stairs, assuming we had a change in fishing plans. The somber faces of the captain, fishing master and Kazukisan greeted me.

The captain motioned me over to the table and tapped a paper lying on its surface. I recognized it as my radio message of the previous day.

Very politely, the captain said "Miss Dairusan, what this mean?" He pointed to a sentence at the end of the report that read, "Please tell me if I should anticipate transfer to another vessel." NMFS had originally told me to expect a possible transfer after three weeks, and this was the end of my third week on the *Kyowa*. I wanted to know what the program had in store for me.

I explained to the captain and fishing master, with Kazuki attempting to interpret, what this sentence meant. The fishing master and captain spoke rapidly to each other. Kazukisan shifted from foot to foot and refused to meet my gaze. The captain poked him and pointed at me. My original cheerfulness disappeared into the tension that hung in the air, a tension that I did not understand.

"Miss Dairusan, maybe you leave because you think we do bad things?" Kazukisan asked sadly.

"Bad things"—what did this mean? How could asking NMFS about a transfer mean I thought the *Kyowa* was doing "bad things?" My confusion deepened. I assured Kazuki that I thought they were doing honest work and I only wanted to know if NMFS wanted me to go to another boat. This time, in their agitated conversation, I heard the words "Coast Guard."

"Maybe you say this to make Coast Guard come on *Kyowa*

because you think we do bad things?" Kazukisan looked at me gravely, sweat beads lining his upper lip. My heart pounded wildly, wondering what kind of confrontation we were heading for. Never before had I experienced any kind of conflict with these men. We worked side by side, easily and happily, day in and day out. We laughed together and teased each other endlessly. These men were my friends. But herein lay the rub. These men were not my friends; we were on opposing sides in a billion dollar business venture. Friendship and loyalty, kindness and consideration would fall away in an instant if I uncovered any wrongdoing by the *Kyowa* and attempted to report it. In their eyes, the entire purpose of my job was to hamper their efforts to catch as much fish as possible. If not for me, would they be throwing back the valuable king crab, halibut and salmon that they caught? Wouldn't they be more likely to underreport their catch sizes so they could catch more fish and make more money than the regulations allowed?

Again, I explained about the possibility of my transferring to another boat. Again, I tried to explain that this line meant nothing other than what it read. I asked Kazukisan why they were concerned about this sentence.

"Miss Dairusan, we know observers have secret word they send to fish boss in Seattle when boats do bad things. Usually word is name of fish. What is this 'anticipate?' It is unusual name of fish? Maybe like shark? It is not on special list." Kazukisan nodded at the captain, and he pulled a book from the shelf over our heads. Flipping through it, he found a tablet size piece of paper folded in half. He opened it and pressed it flat onto the tabletop.

I looked down and saw, painstakingly written out in all capital letters, the exact codes that, even now, sat in my cabin, wedged in a toilet paper roll. My stomach clenched in disbelief. Where they had gotten this list? In the back of my mind, I felt a thrust of panic trying to leap the barrier I had created for it; this barrier that kept all of my fears and doubts contained and manageable. This barrier that had successfully prevented me from considering the possibility that I was now facing: help was *not* just a radio message away. I had no allies out here; I was truly and totally alone.

"These words . . . how did you get these?" I pointed to the list, wondering if Kazuki would tell me.

He conferred with the captain and fishing master and replied, "Fishing master, he get from radio master of *Shotoku Maru*." In an evening radio session, the *Shotoku Maru* had probably shared the codes with all the Japanese boats that were on the air at the time. I marveled at my own naiveté in thinking that my little observer codes would have remained a secret in such a big money industry. With so much at stake, nothing would escape the attention of the officers.

Luckily I had my Japanese/English dictionary with me. I opened it to the word "anticipate," and placed it on the table, pointing to the definition. All three men huddled over the page, talking among themselves. Finally, they straightened up. A red flush crept over Kazukisan's once strained and white face. Both the captain and fishing master bowed deeply, repeating apologies over and over.

"Did you send this message yesterday as normally scheduled?" I glared at the captain, remembering NMFS's strong warning that it was mandatory for us to submit our weekly messages on time.

More bowing and flushed faces. The fishing master spoke harshly to Kazuki, who grabbed my radio message and fled from the bridge, rushing, I assumed, to the radio operator's cabin to have my message sent a day late.

What would have happened if I had been attempting to send in one of my codes? Would the officers have tried to prevent me? Legally, they could do nothing. But laws and legality felt very far removed from the world in which we existed. A tale that I had kept behind my newly ruptured safety barrier seeped through the barrier's break and into my mind: Larry, my friend who had gotten me into this in the first place, had worked on one Japanese ship that developed an elaborate method of secretly freezing pans of fish in an area unknown to the observer. Day after day, Larry's catch estimates differed significantly from the captain's DCCL. He and the captain spent hours going through the logs, the captain innocently scratching his head and insisting that Larry must be making continuous mistakes in his work. It took Larry weeks of sleuthing, but he finally stumbled across the secret area where the crew stashed the unrecorded fish. When he confronted the captain with his discovery, the captain first cried and begged Larry to pretend he had not seen this. Men's livelihoods—their families—depended on this being a successful venture. When this didn't work, and Larry forced the captain to send his message, the entire ship's complement stopped speaking to him and exited rooms as soon as he entered. Larry endured several long and depressing days before the Coast Guard finally boarded and removed him.

It was impossible to think of the fishing master not speaking to me. Impossible to imagine Masadru leaving the dining room when I entered. Or Kazukisan, turning from me when I smiled at him in the factory. Yet I knew all of these things—and more—would occur if I discovered the *Kyowa* cheating and had to report it. Anger, hostility, threats—perhaps even the need to use the now laughable code four.

I felt shaken and jarred. In a matter of minutes, I learned that I had only myself to rely on. That NMFS and the Coast Guard belonged in that other world of laws and legality that did not exist out here and that, despite their assurances, was clearly not easily accessible to me. This was it—my worst fear realized—it was me and me alone out here.

As I continued to work on foreign boats, this very fear became my strength. I learned to trust myself, physically and emotionally and intuitively. I learned to rely on my instincts about people and situations. I developed a solid inner strength that, I think, comes only from self-reliance.

Four years later, when I was traveling alone in Indonesia, this inner strength saved my life. On the island of Lombok, I became extremely ill. In the course of a few hours, I could not even move from the tiny bed on which I lay in a local guest house.

OK, this is bad, I tell myself, but it will pass; I had all of my travel shots, so just give it time. I sweat and shiver and doze. Nickel-sized blisters break out all over my body, oozing clear fluid onto my drenched sheets. A sledgehammer pounds my head. I feel like I have just had my wisdom teeth taken out; then my lower jaw locks up completely and I cannot open my mouth. Hours pass and all I want to do is lie still and not move again, ever, ever. Rest and peace, that is all I want. I have no strength and feel as if I am floating. Somehow, I know if I do not get up and find help, I will never leave this bed and its seductive comfort. I reach deep into my inner core, telling myself that I can sit up. Count to ten, then do it. No? OK, try again. I have to do this, *there is no one here to help me*. Deep breaths, visualize my strength, rely on myself. Slowly, I sit up. Good, very good. See? I, alone, did this. I can do anything. Turn inward: solid steel, that is what I am made of as I stand slowly and painfully. My steel core forces my blistered feet painfully across the cement floor and to the door. I hobble into the dirt street and collapse, just as a donkey cart ambles past. The driver stops and approaches me, a heap near his rear wheel. He is half my size, so I grasp the cart for support, my inner voice commanding me to get up and into the wagon. Now unconsciousness subdues the voice in my head, the one that comes from my place of deep strength.

I awake in a hospital, an IV in my arm and dozens of brown faces peering into my own. My head no longer aches and the fever is gone. I can open my mouth. I smile with the knowledge that I have saved myself.

SEVEN

Man Overboard

ONE AFTERNOON, AS I HEAVED MY BASKETS AROUND IN THE FACTORY, the alarm bells suddenly started ringing. Knee-deep in the beginning of a trawl we had just brought on, I knew the officers could not be ready to re-set the net. Despite the noises of the factory equipment, I heard the fishing master's voice, sounding frantic, over the loudspeaker. Akihamasan stopped his work and motioned for the rest of the crew to follow as he raced up to the deck. Flinging knives aside, men shouted and bumped into each other as they rushed to follow Akihama.

I gave the crew time to clear the stairwells, then went above deck myself. Early afternoon dusk was settling over the ship and the sea shone like a silvery mirror as I emerged from the factory. This far north in the winter, we had daylight only from about 10 a.m. until 3 p.m. I came out on the port side of the deck to find most of the crew clustered against the starboard railing, looking into the water. Several men threw ropes back and forth. Agitated shouts followed the ropes through the air. Seeing the deck master with a life ring in his hand, I realized someone had gone overboard. The deck master threw the life ring, attached to a coiled rope, over the side of the *Kyowa*. I saw two other Japanese fishing boats racing towards us, white waves cresting as their bows pushed through the ocean.

I ran over to the starboard rail, blocked by a pile of fishing net. Climbing to the top of the netting, I grasped the rail to steady myself. In the dimming light, I saw two men in the sea. Their arms flailed through the air, splashing weakly in the water, like tiny young birds, fluttering helplessly because they have not yet learned to fly. One man bobbed under, then slowly rose again. I recognized Masadru, his curls drooping like limp tentacles over his face. The second man, Hoshii, churned the water as he spun in slow circles, round and round. Two life rings floated gently near the men, but neither seemed to notice them. The only clear thought I had was that the water must be terribly, horribly cold.

A splash from midships tore my attention away from the nightmare below me. A life raft containing both the chief officer and the deck master had been lowered into the sea.

The chief officer struggled to start the engine of the rubber dingy. Hoshii had managed to throw an arm over one of the life rings. Masadru sank again beneath the water. Time seemed to stop; surely an hour passed before he rose again. The life boat engine sputtered and died, once, twice, three times. With this, the deck master dove into the frigid water and began swimming—so slowly, it seemed—toward Masadru. He stroked in slow motion—was I dreaming?—through the gently rolling water, grabbing the life ring as he passed it. An hour, two hours passed, before the deck master reached Masadru. He struggled with Masadru's limp body, placing an arm over the life ring; it slid off into the water. The second arm wrapped around the deck master's neck, pulling him under. A wrestling match taking place in the sea, with both contestants sure to lose.

The zodiac engine finally chugged to life, and the chief officer raced first to Hoshii. Leaning precariously over the side, he grabbed Hoshii around the waist and tugged him into the boat, where he lay flopped onto the bottom, not moving. The rescue vessel tilted wildly as the chief officer dove to the back and opened the throttle of the engine, leaping through the water like a giant orange lion springing after its weakened prey.

Another eternity passed before the chief officer succeeded in getting Masadru and the deck master into the life raft, where they joined Hoshii, spread-eagled on the bottom. The chief officer gunned the engine and steered his way back to our vessel. He clipped the two hooks dangling over the side of the ship onto the front and back ends of the life raft. At his signal, the crew member operating the winch slowly began to raise the life raft up and over the side of the *Kyowa*, back onto the deck, where it landed with a thunk.

Several crew members surrounded the life raft and gently picked up both Masadru and Hoshii. Akihamasan, his arms around Masadru, set him upright, but he immediately collapsed onto the deck. The deck master wobbled to his feet, and the crew members bundled the three wet and freezing men off toward the cabins.

I joined a group of milling crew members, including Kazukisan. Gesturing expansively, he explained what had happened. Hoshii had been near the edge of the deck and a wildly swinging cargo hook had knocked him overboard. Masadru had been operating the crane controlling the cargo hook and was the only person who saw what happened. He leapt down from the crane and jumped overboard to try and save Hoshii. Luckily, others saw him jump over, realized what had happened, and sounded the alarm bells.

The deck bell pealed through the air, and Akihamasan motioned for the crew to return to the factory. Reluctantly, they began to make their way down the deck, toward the factory stairs, talking agitatedly among themselves.

I went up to the bridge. Opening the door, I found the fishing master puffing away on a cigarette and swallowing big gulps of Saki. The captain shouted excitedly into the radio, gesturing largely with one hand and holding his own glass of Saki in the other. When he saw me, the captain put down the radio receiver and motioned for me to join him at the chart table. He pointed first at Dutch Harbor and then to Anchorage.

"Mr. Hoshiisan bad hurt shoulder. Maybe, Miss Dairusan, you to call Coast Guard take him to United States hospital. OK?" I knew that the *Kyowa's* chief officer was our only source of First Aid, and his knowledge was minimal—limited, from what I could gather, to band-aids and aspirin. I told the captain I would do whatever I could to help.

Later that evening, the captain told me that I would not need to call the Coast Guard, as there was a Japanese "mother ship" in the area, and we would rendezvous with it. Crew members had provided me with vivid descriptions of these mother ships, or "mamasans," as they called them; they carried supplies of all kinds, as well as doctors and other personnel. All the small fishing boats, like the *Kyowa*, off-loaded their frozen fish products onto the mother ship when their holds were full.

The evening was unusually calm for mid-March in the Bering Sea. Instead of icy winds and sleet, the air stood still and quiet. A wet, chill fog enveloped us. The deck lights shimmered in the soft mist. Water droplets clung to every surface, and they danced in the light like a quivering diamond necklace.

I stood on the flying bridge, the open deck on top of the bridge and the highest point on the vessel. The dampness seeped through my thick layers of clothing. The mist surrounded me like a protective cocoon as I stared out over the dark sea at the blurred lights of other fishing boats in the distance. The sound of foghorns moaned through the night. I felt immersed in an eerie and alien world.

The *Kyowa*'s engines chugged quietly as we made our way through the still water. Suddenly, a huge, dark shape loomed ahead of us, shining softly through the fog. The ethereal mamasan, bigger than I could have imagined. It seemed to have no beginning and no end and shimmered over us like a higher being. Surely it would swallow the *Kyowa*, pulling us right into its vast glow. My own "Abducted by Aliens" adventure.

The men scurried around two stories below me, readying the life raft for Hoshii. Their words echoed and bounced through the darkness. I imagined that we must look like a tiny insect beside the mamasan's vast, impenetrable hull. Craning my neck upward, I could see lights and shadowy, small figures leaning out over the deck. They seemed miles above me.

Our crewmen lowered the lifeboat overboard, with Hoshii and the chief officer ensconced. The chief officer motored to the waiting mamasan and attached long, dangling cables to his raft. Slowly, slowly, the small boat began to climb up the steep side of the large vessel. I watched as it passed the *Kyowa*'s bridge, and then me, crawling like a small bug up and up the dark hull and disappearing over the top.

Still later that night—or rather, early morning—the chief officer returned alone to the *Kyowa*. Hoshii was to be sent back home on the next boat returning to Japan, as his injury was too serious to be treated at sea.

On the bridge, the fishing master told me that the next net would not be set until later in the morning. I returned to my cabin and fell into bed. I tossed restlessly on my sandbag mattress, feeling small and alone. The sea allowed us to encase ourselves in steel and float upon her surface; she even shared with us the offerings of her depths. Then it was as if she needed to remind us that we were here at her invitation, an invitation that could be revoked at any time. A storm, a person overboard . . . with these the sea showed her power over us.

I envisioned standing on the stern deck of the *Kyowa* at night as we churned through the water to a new fishing area, stumbling accidentally over a coil of net, and flailing over the side into the darkness, down, down into the cold black sea. Watching the *Kyowa* as it raced away from me, no one having seen me. I wondered how long I would last in that dark, horribly cold water? Ten minutes, maybe. It was a long time before I fell asleep.

EIGHT

My Fair Lady

I AWOKE, STARTLED, TO THE BUZZING OF THE SMALL TELEPHONE IN my cabin. Leaning over the edge of my bunk, I picked it up and said, "Moshi, Moshi!," the telephone greeting Masadru had taught me.

"Miss Dairusan, we are approaching the edge of the ices. Come please here." I recognized the voice of the captain.

My morning ritual consisted of throwing on every piece of warm clothing I had and braving my way onto the deck. I liked to check the weather and the state of the crew. Sometimes while I slept, the world passed me by. Nets were set, trawls pulled on, work begun and completed. All while I snoozed away, dreaming of solid ground and Hagan-Daaz ice cream.

Blasting cold slammed me in the face as I stepped out onto the deck. In the warm living quarters of the ship, it was sometimes easy to forget the harsh conditions of the outside world. I squinted my eyes at the glaring scene: mountains of ice like thick, swirled frosting on a cake covered every surface, a foot thick in places. Shiny, hard ice coated the handrails, the coiled nets and the tall masts. Upside down icicles poked out from odd places, frozen into demonic shapes by the fierce Arctic wind. Teetering above me, crew members with axes chopped away at the icy build up that threatened to make the *Kyowa* top heavy.

A careful balancing act is required to keep a ship from capsizing. Each boat has a specific degree of tilt that it can comfortably roll without going over. If this margin of error is exceeded, the ship can easily capsize. Which is why, I had come to understand, the freezer men were very careful about stacking the 25 kilogram boxes of frozen fish in specific areas of the fish hold. The weight that the ship carried as we filled up our hold had to be carefully managed.

The men struggled to stay afoot on the icy deck as the wind buffeted them about like skidding ping pong balls. I noticed safety lines tied around their waists. Since the men-overboard accident, this had, thankfully, become standard practice. Ice glittered and danced as the men chopped away.

I watched this Holiday on Ice spectacular until my face turned numb from the cold, then went up to the bridge. Checking the loran, I saw that our position was 60° 26.22' North and 178°55.76' West—the same latitude as St. Matthew and Nunivak Islands.

The captain and the fishing master greeted me, pointing ahead into the bright distance. I saw what looked like a vast, shimmering snow field. Grabbing the powerful bridge binoculars, I squinted through them. I could make out, in some spots, individual chunks of ice.

"We go there because many fishes," the captain said.

I looked up the word "danger" in my dictionary and pointed it out to them; they both laughed. They often seemed to laugh at what I rarely considered funny—including approaching a vast field of ice in a 150-foot boat. After all, hadn't the *Titanic* been sunk by icebergs? It was a heck of a lot bigger than our bathtub of a boat. I wrote the word "Titanic" on paper and imitated a sinking ship; they only laughed harder.

Just then, Akihama passed by the bridge window, pickax in hand—he had come from above on the flying bridge, chopping away the ice build up. I sketched an icy, top heavy ship plowing into an iceberg for the captain and the fishing master. Naturally, this sent them off into another fit of laughter.

I threw up my hands in frustration and went off to the galley to have breakfast. If I was going down, I would go on a full stomach.

Two hours later, I felt the ship hesitate, then shudder for several seconds. And again—hesitate, then shudder, rather like a car being forced to accelerate before the engine was fully warmed up. Each time we shuddered, I heard faint crunching sounds. I thought of Rice Crispies crackling in a bowl of milk.

I raced up to the bridge. The ocean had become a carpet of trembling ice. Ice all around, filling my field of vision, dancing and bobbing like huge styrofoam pieces, seemingly weightless in the water. Clouds had moved in, and the silvery sea mirrored the sky. Like snowflakes, no two icebergs appeared the same. The pristine whiteness of the ice mixed with beautiful Arctic blue streaks, clean and crisp and frozen into strange shapes. One looked like the wrinkled face of an old man, his flowing beard that brilliant opaque blue. In another I could see an elephant, the massive body sloping into the head and trunk. Yet another resembled a group of faces, their features blurred and indistinct.

I looked on the fish finder and even my untrained eye easily spotted the red blob that indicated a large school of *mintai*. The crew set the net. After only an hour, they pulled it back in, displacing bobbing chunks of ice as they reeled the stuffed net through the water and onto the deck. All day, as we worked in the factory, our bodies thudded with the eerie shuddering and vibrating of the ship.

*   *   *

Several mornings later, the sun beamed down and I raised my face to the sky, soaking up its warmth, a bear emerging from hibernation. The icebergs seemed like a dream. The fresh warm breeze carried a salty tang and a slight hint of springtime. I envisioned narcissus blossoms, delicate in the spring sun, their intoxicating odor wafting over me.

Leaning over the deck railing, I gazed down upon a dozen dolphins as they chased and played alongside the boat. In my next life, I hope to come back as a dolphin; I dream of dancing through the water with their grace and ease. I smiled as they cavorted and whistled to each other, their movements a beautiful water ballet.

Suddenly, over the loudspeaker came the sounds of the classic song "Barbara Ann," by The Beach Boys.

"Ba-ba-ba, Ba-ba-baran!! Bar-ba-rannnnnn . . ." the music blared, filling the air.

Spontaneously, I started dancing. The men stopped their work on deck and stared at me in open mouthed amazement. I bounced over and grabbed both Kazuki and Akihama by the hands, pulling them into my wild dance. The three of us twisted and laughed and tried to sing along—the only words we could manage were the "Ba-ba-bas." Soon the entire deck crew surrounded us, clapping and laughing. A couple of other men joined in our dance, following us as we sashayed around stacked nets and coiled cables, kicking our steel-toed boots high into the air. We grinned happily as we twirled past each other. On the bridge, the fishing master captured the scene with his video camera. I laughed out loud at the odd juxtaposition of dancing with Japanese men on a fishing boat in the Bering Sea to the strains of American rock and roll.

The impromptu deck dancing session was the talk of the ship all day. When I went to the bridge that evening, Kazuki, Akihama, the captain and fishing master chattered excitedly.

"Miss Dairusan, you very good dancer!" Kazuki blushed, as he still often did when he spoke to me, even after a month.

"Oh, Kazukisan, YOU are very good dancer. So is Akihamasan."

Akihama spoke up "Miss Dairusan, Mr. Kazukisan, he is fever dancer! At home, he goes to discos and all night he fever dances!"

Kazuki, of course, blushed more fiercely. Turning the attention away from himself, he pointed to the fishing master and said, "Fishing master is champion singer and 1-2-3 dancer!"

Anything but shy, the fishing master smiled slyly at me. He put on some slow Japanese music, approached me and bowed. He took both of my hands and we twirled around the tiny bridge. He repeated, "One-two-sree, one-two-sree . . ." as we moved rhythmically along. We swept by the fish finder, the loran unit, the chart table. As we brushed by the radio, the voices of other Japanese fishermen crackled over the soft, soothing sound of the dance music.

The song ended, and we stopped our dance. The other men applauded us. After showing off his "1-2-3" dance skills, the fishing master now wanted to teach me some Japanese songs. I was eager to learn, despite my terrible singing voice.

The fishing master rigged up a reel-to-reel tape deck and hand held microphone. He placed earphones on his head. Beautiful music filled the air, and the fishing master began singing . . . "Hanasaki Min-a-to." At this point, I had never heard of Karoake, and this was well before the "Karoake Craze" hit the States. I thought it a bit odd that he seemed to be lip-synching the song.

Kazuki told me the song was about saying good-bye to a departing fishing vessel. He described a poignant scene as the wives and children of the fishermen gather on the dock with banners and streamers to see them off, tears all around. Having learned that most Japanese men go to sea for six to nine months and return home for only a month or two between trips, I could easily understand why an entire farewell song would be written about this experience.

Next it was my turn. The fishing master had a copy of the words written, not in Japanese symbols but in the English alphabet, which made them phonetically easy for me to read. They hooked me up and turned on the music. Through my headphones, I heard the lilting voice of a woman singing the haunting song. I sang along as best I could, stumbling over many of the words. Now catching on to this Karoake thing, I realized my small audience was not hearing the talented singer, but instead the cracking, off-key voice of yours truly. Somehow, I thought it worked like a choir—my voice blending with and being superseded by the more beautiful voice. God, this was embarrassing. Worse than my first day on the boat when I kept throwing up in front of them. I warbled out the last note of the song, and the men clapped and cheered and assured me it had been beautiful. Right.

After "singing," Kazuki and I worked on our language lessons. We had been exchanging vocabulary words over the past month and I learned a good many, but grammar and sentence structure seemed beyond me. The fishing master, never one to remain in the background, suddenly interrupted us with a torrent of monotone words:

"I get up at six in the morning I wash my face and my hands." He beamed proudly at me. My mouth fell open in amazement;

this from a man whose only English words I had heard were "yes" and "oh nice." Kazuki told me this was all the fishing master remembered from his grade school English lessons.

Kazuki began telling me the Japanese names for various animals. To identify each animal, we imitated their sound.

"Moo-oo-oo!" (Cow/*ushi*).

"Neigh—neigh!" (Horse/*uma*).

"Woof! Woof!" (Dog/*inu*)

I brayed out a rooster crow, "Cock-a-doodle-do!," and the men stared at me. Again I cock-a-doodle-dooed. Akihamasan poked Kazuki and rolled his eyes.

"Miss Dairusan, please what is this strange animal? I think we not have one in Japan. Maybe only in America. And, please, you to make that sound again!" The captain grinned, encouraging me.

Another "cock-a-doodle-do" sent them off into gales of laughter. The fishing master removed his glasses to wipe his eyes. I looked up the word for rooster and pointed it out to the captain.

"Oh—*niwatori*!" He identified it to the other three, and, simultaneously, they all sing-songed "Ko-ki-ko-ko! Ko-ki-ko-ko!"

It was my turn to laugh. Listen to a rooster sometime. Then decide if you hear a "doodle."

*   *   *

After my way-off-Broadway performance, I couldn't believe the men eagerly invited me to sing for them again the following evening on the bridge. I decided they were tone deaf or masochists. I squeaked my way through "Hanasaki-min-a-to" and then the talk turned to our lives at home.

Early in the voyage, I thought the captain did not speak English. I had discovered, however, that he was simply shy.

"Captain, do you have family?" Instead of blushing, as I was afraid he might, he whipped out a photograph of a woman holding a tiny baby and proudly pointed at each, saying "wife . . . son."

He eagerly unfolded the story of his marriage for me. At 32, his parents grew concerned about his lack of a wife. His mother put out the word that her son needed a spouse. A family neighbor found a bride for the captain, in the old Japanese tradition of *mia*, an arranged marriage. He became engaged, and went to sea for five months. He returned home to marry the woman he hardly knew, then had to go to work again, this time for six months.

The captain looked at me and shrugged ruefully, raising his hands and eyebrows. He had been to sea for most of his married life. His son had been born five days before he left on this trip four months ago, and he had not seen his family since.

I asked him if he was happy this way. Again, he shrugged and half-smiled at me, his large brown eyes seeming to hold a world of sorrow.

"Miss Dairusan, I not very happy. But is OK—now I have baby son. That is good." His gaze dropped to the photograph in his hand.

The fishing master, eager to tell me of his personal life, brought out a stack of photographs. Thinking they were of his family, I began to thumb through them. Young Japanese women with demure smiles gazed at me.

"Kazukisan, these are fishing master's daughters?" I looked questioningly at both of them. Kazukisan translated for the fishing master and he guffawed loudly. Kazuki, as usual, blushed. The fishing master prodded him, encouraging him to explain the joke to me.

"Uh, Miss Dairusan, ummm . . . these girls not daughter. These girls . . . ummm . . ." Kazuki's blush spread from his face to his neck. "These girls are sweethearts for fishing master." Sweat popped on his forehead.

Poor Kazukisan. My curiosity, however, outweighed my sympathy. "But what about the fishing master's wife? Does she know about girlfriends?"

"Oh, yes. She never mind. Many fishing men have lots of sweethearts." A succinct answer.

From what I had learned in talking with the men on the ship, their relationships with their wives were often ones of convenience. Each person played a certain role to make the marriage work, operating in her/his own sphere. I gathered there was tremendous pressure to marry and produce children. Hence, if someone was not married by a certain age, *mia*, a marriage was arranged. I wondered what the wives of these men thought; what did they feel about their husbands being away at sea so much of the time? Perhaps being separated was not such a bad thing for them. I knew that wives were expected to wait on their husbands and be totally subservient to them. Maybe having their mates away afforded them some freedom.

Though I loved my boat and enjoyed a wonderful rapport with the crew, I knew the only reason I received such good treatment was because I was a foreign—*gaigen*—woman. Had I been a Japanese woman, my experience would have been entirely different. For one thing, I would never be aboard the *Kyowa*. The men took seriously the idea that women bring bad luck. I know it was difficult for many of the men to adjust to having a woman on board. Even after two months, several of the men would still not return my greetings. Two of them refused to even look me in the eye.

One night in the galley, a conversation I had with Masadru gave me a first hand glimpse into the men's thinking.

"Miss Dairusan, *Otoku* (men) are kings, *Ona* (women) are inferior." Masadru spoke earnestly.

"Now, Masadru, why is that?" I wanted to thump his curly head but refrained.

"Because what kind of work *Ona* do? No work. *Ona* only make babies and stay home all day. Easy. We *Otoku* everyday hard work. Everyday must be strong, never weak like *Ona*." He pounded the table emphatically.

"Masadru, if women did not have babies, you would not even BE here! And you don't mean to tell me that you think your wife—with three young children at home—sits around all day?!" I flailed my arms, a bad sign.

"Yes, yes! She sit around all day! Just like you say!" Masadru nodded in what he thought was agreement.

"No, no, no—that is not what I meant. Your wife does not sit around all day! In fact, she probably RUNS around all day, chasing after your children. She's probably exhausted from taking care of them. And what does she do when you come home?" It took a bit of explaining for him to understand my question.

"My wife, she love me home. Everyday, she do what I say. She bring me beer, she make my bath, she cook my food. She happy when I home."

I swallowed hard. "What about your children? Do you help with them?"

"I play with my children then give them back to her. Her job, not mine, change diaper, feed them." He scowled manfully.

I stood up to leave the room, the only reasonable action I could take. Smacking Masadru would be unreasonable.

Masadru and the fishing master, though they were both generous and kind to me, seemed to have the most difficulty with my "non-feminine" ways. Both were convinced that I had no husband because of my behavior. My insistence that I did not *want* a husband was beyond their comprehension. One morning on the bridge, they tried to deliver a Japanese version of "My Fair Lady."

"Miss Dairusan, you must be talking more quiet. To get husband, you must speak in soft voice like this." Masadru batted his eyelashes and mumbled a few unintelligible words. "When you greet *Otoku*, you must bow down." He demonstrated, kneeling before the fishing master, saying in falsetto, "*Ohayo Gozaimas.*"

Playing along, I knelt before the 5' tall Masadru and shrilly said, "*Ohayo Gozaimas.*" Throwing caution and cultural respect to the wind, I clasped my arms around his legs and quickly hoisted his light frame into the air, throwing him over my shoulder before he could resist. I paraded around the bridge, shouting in a deep voice "*Ohayo Goziamas!*"

The captain collapsed against the chart table, screaming with laughter. Kazukisan stood stunned, his mouth hanging open. Throwing open a cupboard door, the fishing master whipped out his video camera and followed me around while Masadru thrashed against my back. As I stomped by the bridge window, Masadru grabbed the roll bar beside it and yanked us both backwards like a rubber band. I slowly lowered him to the floor, fully expecting him to be livid.

His eyes like saucers, he had only one query. "Miss Dairusan, how you do that?"

"Masadru," I said, "In my country, women big and strong. *Ona* great, *Otoku* no great. *Otoku* afraid of *Ona*. Now you see why!"

Fortunately, this put an end to any further attempts by either Masadru or the fishing master to "tame" me. As with the deck dancing, however, the ship buzzed with news of this latest craziness of the *gaigen* observer. That afternoon in the factory, Kazukisan and Akihamasan approached my work station. Akihama stood behind Kazukisan and lifted him off his feet then placed him gently back on the floor.

He said "Now you, Miss Dairusan!"

Rolling my eyes, I picked up a pliant Kazukisan and, for good measure, swung him around in a tight circle. We were both lucky I didn't slip in the fish slime and crash down on top of him.

At this point, men turned off their electric saws and put down their knives. The entire crew gathered around my work station to watch. Someone shouted "Again! Again!" Once more, I lifted a blushing Kazukisan into the air. The men shouted among themselves, daring each other to be next. No one rose to the challenge, so reluctantly we all returned to our work.

For days, men kept picking each other up in front of me. They would stack two baskets full of fish on top of each other and try to get me to pick them up. They lugged heavy objects to my work station and did the same, gathering around and urging me to show off my prowess. Feeling I now had a point to prove, I would show off by picking up those objects not heavy enough for injury. For good measure, I would occasionally grab one of the smaller men and lift him off his feet. This always caused howls of laughter from those around us and requests for "Again! Again!"

*　　*　　*

One morning, after I had been on the *Kyowa* for eight weeks, the radio officer brought me a message from NMFS. He smiled at me sadly, saying, "Miss Dairusan, I think you must to go now."

Indeed, the message stated that the program had arranged for me to return to Dutch Harbor on another Japanese fishing vessel that was making the rounds and taking several observers back at once. I needed to contact the ship, the *Shotoku Maru*, and coordinate a rendezvous as soon as possible.

Conflicting emotions filled me. The *Kyowa* was comfortable and familiar, and I wasn't sure I was ready to go. I thought of what I would be leaving. No more singing sessions on the bridge. I wouldn't be able to pick up Kazukisan and swing him around anymore, causing everyone to ooh and ahh and boost my ego. Dancing on the deck, my laughter joining that of Masadru and Akihama. What if my next boat was full of sullen sailors and hostile officers? I remembered the stories of prior observers. I thought of the NMFS program staff, to whom I would have to present and defend my data. I compared my nervousness at this prospect to my nervousness when my first trawl came on board. My confidence had increased with every trawl, and I felt sure that most of my data would be acceptable. I tried to recall what it was like to wake up and go for a bicycle ride instead of putting on a dank, smelly rainsuit and wading through stacks of flopping fish.

"Miss Dairusan, I think *Shotoku* not far. Speak to captain. I wish you not to leave. We miss you." The radio officer broke into my thoughts.

On the bridge, the captain and I raised the *Shotoku Maru* on the radio. The *Shotoku* sat at anchor east of us, less than a day away. I left the captain making transfer arrangements and rushed off to the factory to begin cleaning and packing my gear, grabbing my rain gear from the changing room on the way.

My baskets sat neatly stacked beside my work bench. Every crevice of their criss-cross openings oozed with slime. Plastic forms covered in fish scales and pencil marks leaned against them. I jiggled the hanging scales, hoping to shake off some of the debris.

I unstacked my baskets and spread them out on the factory floor. Turning on the sea water hose, I aimed it at the baskets. The water shot out with the force of a fire hose, and the baskets sped across the floor like entries in a boxcar derby. The winner ended up under the conveyor belt, tipped upside down. The losers crashed into various corners of the factory. I chased them down one by one, this time planting a foot in each as I hosed them down. Using Comet cleanser, I attacked the baskets with a stiff bristled brush. No matter how much I scrubbed, minuscule bits of fish and guts clung to every opening.

Once the baskets seemed a bit closer to their true shade of blue, I spread my rain gear out on a conveyor belt. Fondly, I recalled the first day I paraded around in my cheerful yellow suit. Now an outfit of dull green, spattered with globs of brown and gray, stared back at me. I dumped cleanser on my once proud uniform and swiped away. Hanging both the jacket and pants up to drip dry, I headed to the bridge to check the status of my transfer.

The captain and the fishing master stood at their usual posts and greeted me wistfully.

"Miss Dairusan, we miss you very much. You are *Kyowa*'s most best observer!" The captain ducked his head, blushing.

"I get up at six in the morning I wash my face and my hands yes oh nice!" The fishing master blurted out every word of English that he knew, smiling proudly. He then spoke in Japanese to the captain.

"Miss Dairusan, fishing master have gift for you." The captain nodded back at him.

The fishing master opened a cabinet above his head and carefully pulled down a tall glass case, setting it on the chart table, saying "Oh nice!"

I walked slowly over, trying to identify the item in the middle of the display case. A true vision in white returned my curious stare—a Japanese wedding doll. The porcelain bride had intricately painted hair complete with tiny lacquered chopsticks. Her silk kimono fell in soft swirls and trailed out behind her. The hands of the doll were folded demurely in front of her, and her eyes gazed downward. The perfect gift for a failed "My Fair Lady."

"*Arigato*! Thank you so much." I smiled at my friend, the fishing master. For good measure, he placed two pairs of cellophane-wrapped pantyhose on top of the case. At least I knew my friend Dyanne could use these to stake up her garden tomatoes.

"Miss Dairusan, we wrap doll for you. I have Kazukisan fix for airplane ride, no problem." The captain picked up the telephone and rang Kazukisan.

All day, crew members stopped by my cabin and gave me farewell gifts. Masadru presented me with a pair of thick warm socks, telling me I would need them when I worked on a Russian boat, as he heard they had no heat. The blushing face of Kazukisan peered into my cabin as I bent over my duffel, stuffing data forms into it.

"Miss Dairusan, please, for you." He hesitantly placed a small framed photograph in my hand. A smiling Kazuki stood surrounded by his family, under cherry trees in full blossom. "My family go to Kyoto to see cherry trees last year." I wanted so much to hug Kazuki, but I knew he would probably collapse at my feet if I did. I settled instead for a handshake and a heartfelt *arigato*.

By 10 p.m., my packed gear sat on the deck, the fragile wedding doll padded and secured in a large box. Masadru, Kazuki and I stood around, laughing and teasing each other. Within a few minutes, Masadru grabbed my sleeve.

"*Shotoku Maru!*" He said, pointing to lights not too distant.

The fishing master announced something over the loudspeaker, and the crew slowly appeared on deck. Within half an hour, we pulled along side the *Shotoku Maru*. In this bay, the water looked calm, but the *Kyowa* still rolled slightly back and forth. I watched as the men dropped big black buoys to be used as fenders, attached to ropes, down the side of the ship. Crewmen on the *Shotoku* tossed lines over to our deck, and the crew began tying the boats together. Innocently, I wondered how I would be transferred to the *Shotoku*.

Just then, I heard a yell from the *Shotoku* and looked to see an

American man waving to me—another observer. We shouted back and forth to each other. Then his eyes widened and he said "Oh, no—look!"

I turned to see the *Kyowa* crew members laying a plank between the two rocking ships. The board was two feet wide and stretched the 15 feet between the *Kyowa* and the *Shotoku Maru*. My God, they were going to make me walk the plank. No, they couldn't— they wouldn't. Would they?

Masadru and Kazuki had tied lines around my bundles of gear. Masadru then went up to the crane and they attached the lines to a cargo hook and swung the gear over to the *Shotoku*. I waited for the doll to come loose from the hook and either splash into the water or crash onto the deck. Amazingly, everything landed softly and safely on the opposite deck.

The fishing master and the captain motioned to me from the end of the plank. My stomach in knots, I walked slowly over, refusing to believe what I knew they would tell me.

"Miss Dairusan, we tie line around you. Easy for you to cross to *Shotoku* on this wood. Ocean is very still." The captain looked at me encouragingly, just as the *Kyowa* rolled to starboard.

I had no room in my flutter of fear to feel sadness about leaving my friends, and I could barely say good-bye. Masadru tied a safety line around my waist, and I stood numbly in front of the plank. The fishing master tugged on my hand, urging me to step onto the board. My legs, once again, had become tree trunks and refused to move. I smiled grimly at him, imagining an eye patch over his left eye and a scraggly black beard surrounding a toothless mouth. Just because I refused to be a lady did not mean I deserved to walk the plank.

The shouts of the observer next door broke into my trance.

"Hey, come on over! The water's fine!" I heard his laughter over the wind.

Taking a deep breath, I stepped out onto the narrow wooden pathway and forced my jelly-like legs to move forward. This fear felt familiar, the same that had possessed me two months ago, when I was leaping through the air, trying to grasp a writhing, snake-like Jacob's ladder. Why did that seem easier than tottering across this wobbly plank? Just as I reached the half-way point, a wave rolled both ships and the board shifted. Panicked, I lost my balance. Arms flailing, I fell onto the hard surface, and my right foot slipped off. I hugged the board as tightly as I could, gasping, but not seeming to take in any air. Terror froze me in place. My eyes locked on the dark water, churning, it seemed, miles below me. I rocked back and forth, welded to my stiff lifeline as it see-sawed up and down. Muffled shouts filtered through the fog surrounding me. Slowly, so slowly, I inched forward along the plank, pulling myself along with my gloved hands. Hours later, my eyes stared down at a wooden deck instead of the angry black sea. I loosened my death grip as hands and arms wrapped around me like tentacles, rolling me off the board now imprinted on my chest. They gently lowered me to the deck of the *Shotoku Maru*, and I lay there, shivering. A white face loomed over me, saying "Are you alright? Are you OK?"

The white face belonged to Tom, the observer, and he helped me to my feet. I shook myself back to reality. Already, the crew was untying us from the *Kyowa*. These guys wasted no time. I tried to pull myself together. I had to wave good-bye to the *Kyowa*.

Tom and I stepped to the deck railing, just as the *Kyowa* inched away from the *Shotoku*. The men lined the railing, waving and shouting to me. I looked at the familiar faces of Masadru, Kazuki, Akihama—even the fishing master had stayed down on the deck. Lifting my gaze to the bridge, I saw the captain waving through the window. I waved back at all of them, shouting "*Arigato*! *Sayanara*!"

As the *Kyowa* turned in the water, the captain sounded the fog horn—once, twice, three times. I continued waving until I could no longer see the faces of my friends.

Tom turned to me and said "Well, that will be something to write home about, won't it?"

I could only agree.

NINE

Orekhova

KNEE-DEEP MUD FILLED THE STREETS OF DUTCH HARBOR. WHENEVER a battered, four-wheel drive vehicle churned through town, buildings, dogs and passers-by received a spattering of wet brown goo. Instead of the arctic white of February—four months ago—the hills rising above town now offered a soft green covering. Tiny wildflowers scattered themselves in the rolling carpet of grass. Their pale colors enhanced the overall softness of Dutch in the springtime.

After the *Kyowa*, I had worked for a month on another Japanese boat, the *Akawa Maru*. Then I spent three weeks in Seattle, "debriefing" from my working cruises. I explained and defended my data collection and wrote a report for each cruise. Program staff checked my forms and had me correct mistakes, of which there were fewer than I had feared. I reviewed my radio messages—they had been received exactly as I sent them, including the sentence about transferring that caused the *Kyowa* so much angst. My debriefing successful, the program assigned me to go back to sea, this time on a Soviet vessel.

In the early afternoon sun, I stood on the deck of a small American catcher boat, the *Excalibur*, traveling through silky calm seas to rendezvous with my Soviet fishing trawler, *MS Orekhova*. The Soviet fishery differed from the Japanese in that most boats operated as joint ventures, working with two or three American catcher boats. The small catcher boats actually set and retrieved the nets of fish, delivering them to the Soviet vessels for processing and freezing. The *Excalibur* worked with the *MS Orekhova* and several other Soviet ships.

In the early 1980s, American fishing vessels couldn't fish on their own as the foreign ships did. Our ships were simply too small to catch, process and freeze the great tonnages of fish handled by the Japanese and Soviets. The purpose of the joint venture fishery with the Soviets was to give our fishers a bigger share of the fish found in American waters. A complicated system of dividing up the profits between the Americans and the Soviets required intensive computer analysis and a good number of staff people to administrate the cash flow.

My thoughts turned to the Soviets. The political system of the Soviet Union had always fascinated me. The idea of a government that treated all of its people equally fed my activist soul. I had some idea that I could change the world, or at least my own country. My idealism loomed large and undisturbed, an escaped helium balloon, sailing brightly through the air. Eventually it would bump against items that would puncture it, dragging it down, until it became just a small scrap of color, no longer soaring, but bouncing and snagging its way along. For now, however, I was convinced that the path to change required, first of all, a system whose main tenants offered everyone a fair chance and equal share, and upheld the responsibility of supporting ALL of its people.

I was also intrigued by the idea that the Soviet Union was forbidden territory. Southern Evangelical churches forbid dancing, card playing and alcohol. This, of course, only tempts one to partake all the more. How can you stay away from something that wields enough power so that others want to deny it to you? I felt the same about the Soviet Union. My curiosity was only strengthened by my government's warnings that the USSR was the "evil empire," the "communist threat."

I read everything I could get my hands on about the Soviet Union, publications from both the left and the right. I believed little of what our government said about the USSR, thinking that most of it was propaganda. After all, these were the years of Reagan paranoia and hostility. Surely conditions in the USSR were exaggerated by a government that needed to keep us afraid of that "communist threat." But I was also skeptical of leftist information—

which, I was convinced, presented a too-perfect-to-be-true picture. With contrasting images in my head, I was eager to learn the truth for myself.

The brief NMFS orientation on life aboard Soviet ships had let me know things would be very different from my Japanese boat. Every Soviet vessel had a political officer onboard, the commissar, whose sole job was to keep the entire ship's complement in line politically. The commissar outranked the captain and was always a man. Though the commissar had no power over me (observers were their own entities), he did over everyone else on the ship and could make life miserable for anyone he felt was "too close" to the observer. The driving force behind the vigilance of the commissar was the fear of defection. If a Soviet learned what life was like outside the Soviet Union, the government was convinced that s/he would immediately attempt to defect. This, of course, was the ultimate humiliation for a country that supposedly provided its people with everything.

By mid-afternoon, the *Excalibur* had reached our meeting spot, and we dropped anchor. In the distance, I could see a large ship making its way toward us, waves of thick black smoke billowing out behind it. More than twice the size of the *Kyowa*, the *Orekhova* threatened to plow us over as it drew near. The ship turned down wind, and choking diesel fumes wrapped around me. The *Orekhova* seemed to radiate neglect, like an old railroad engine that should be in the junkyard. Huge rust stains dotted the hull, dimming the industrial gray paint job. The paint that currently escaped the rust flaked into the water, chips falling like snow as the ship shuddered into position to drop anchor. In sharp contrast to its shabby surroundings, the black smokestack took front and center on the deck. Painted on top, the fire-engine red Soviet flag, with its imposing gold hammer and sickle, gleamed in the sun. It seemed to cast a glow over the entire ship.

I saw many men, and a few women, milling around on the stern deck. Several men worked on detaching one of the bright red life boats from its mooring. I waved and shouted "*Dobry dzien!*" ("Good day" in Russian). Exclaiming among themselves, those who had heard me waved happily back.

Lowered to the sea, the red life boat made its way toward the *Excalibur*. I knew that someone had to be piloting it, though I could see no one, as the boat was all enclosed. It reminded me of a small red submarine with three porthole openings on top. Pulling alongside us, a gruff looking man popped his head through one of these portholes. He looked a bit like a bear wearing a padded green jacket. Wispy gray hair sprang in patches from his cheeks, and a grubby blue wool hat sat on his head. Smiling, I said, "*Dobry dzien*!" His serious face immediately broke into a huge grin, revealing two silver teeth. With the help of a couple of the *Excalibur* crew members, I managed to stuff my blue baskets and duffel bag into one of the portholes. During this flurry of gear stowing, I noticed John, the *Excalibur* second mate, discreetly slip two small brown bags to the lifeboat pilot. He, in turn, pulled a small bundle tightly wrapped in fish netting from his bulky jacket and, keeping his back to the *Orekhova*, gave it to John. I asked John what this was all about. He said his bags contained cigarettes, beer and baseball hats in exchange for Russian vodka from the lifeboat pilot. Interesting—since Gorbachev had come to power, alcohol was supposedly prohibited on all Soviet ships.

"Hey, Dail, did NMFS tell you the scuttlebutt about the *Orekhova*?" John looked at me nonchalantly.

I raised my eyebrows. I knew that this placement was a last minute one, but I assumed it was because an observer had canceled or gotten sick. NMFS had mentioned nothing special about this situation.

"This boat has a real hard-ass commissar. A few weeks ago, the radio officer and his assistant got caught drinking with Carol, the previous observer. The commissar shipped both of 'em back to Russia without so much as a by-your-leave. Carol was so pissed that she threatened to quit unless NMFS shifted her to another boat. We transferred her, which is why I know this stuff." John shook his head. "Just watch yourself and stay out of the way of that asshole commissar."

I couldn't believe that NMFS had not told me this. Of course, they probably figured if I knew the history, I would have refused the ship assignment. And they had to have an observer on the boat in order for it to work in the joint venture fishery; boats were not allowed to take fish unless we were in place.

"Miss! Miss!" I turned away from John to see the lifeboat pilot beckoning. I fleetingly wondered if I should dive headfirst through the porthole. That had been the best way to get my duffel bag in. Taking a deep breath, I stepped onto the top of the lifeboat, grabbing the hand of the pilot as we rocked crazily back and forth. I sat down on the edge of the opening, swinging my legs down into the hole. I waved good-bye to the crew of the *Excalibur* and dropped down to the bottom of the vessel.

As we chugged toward the *Orekhova*, I couldn't see a thing from my seat in the bottom of the boat. I was surprised when we clanged against the hull. With difficulty, the chubby pilot hefted himself through a porthole and onto the top of the lifeboat. He crawled around above me, shouting in Russian and clanking cables into place. With one final shout, we swung wildly through the air as the lifeboat climbed up the side. I braced myself with one hand against the side wall and the other gripping the bench. We thunked onto the deck. The pilot's face appeared above me, peering down through one of the portholes. He motioned for me to come up. I stepped onto the bench and then onto the top of my packed baskets. This gave me just enough height to see out of the porthole. But how was I going to climb through it? I wedged my arms above me and grasped the edges, trying to pull myself up. Even in first grade, I had failed the Phys Ed pull-up exam; this felt like the same contest with the same result. I tried again to heave myself upward with no success.

A second man joined the pilot on top of the lifeboat. He grinned at me, exposing a full row of silver teeth and bent down and grabbed my right arm. The pilot grabbed my left one and together the men hoisted me up, through the porthole and onto the top of the lifeboat. I closed my eyes for just a moment, trying to determine if this was more humiliating than the day I threw up in front of the officers on the *Kyowa*. Before I could decide, the two men tugged at my sleeves and assisted me as I climbed down from the lifeboat and onto the deck of the *Orekhova*.

Four men immediately surrounded me. One shook my hand

vigorously and introduced himself as the captain, Alexander Ivanovitch. A padded green jacket barely contained his imposing girth. Brown polyester pants clung to his stork-like legs. His round face, heavily pock-marked, revealed silver teeth.

My hand felt like it was in a vice grip. I said "*Dobry dzien*—my name is Dail."

His brow wrinkled in concentration. "Hmm . . . Dain . . . Dare . . . what this sound like in Russian? Ahh—Dasha! Your name is Dasha!" He smiled happily.

Pleased to have my Russian name, I thanked him. The second man stepped forward and introduced himself as the chief mate, also shaking my hand with eagerness. A blonde bear, he had a smooth face and soft, wispy hair lay in plastered strips across the top of his head. His blue eyes twinkled. He wore faded blue jeans secured over his paunch with a black belt bearing a gleaming gold buckle. His name was Alexander Mikhailovitch—Sasha.

A tall man next introduced himself as Fyodor Pyotrovitch, the factory manager. Greasy brown hair topped an Ichabod Crane face. His eyes peered through thick glasses with heavy black rims. A navy polyester shirt and brown pants hung crookedly on his thin frame. His smile was tight lipped and his hand, as I shook it, was limp and cold.

I turned to the final man in our small circle. Like those of a bird of prey, his flat, cold, searching eyes were yellow as they locked on my face. A claw-like hand gripped mine tightly as he smiled thinly. I distrusted him immediately. He told me he was Mikhail Alexanderovitch, the first mate. First mate? But I had just met the chief mate. Then I remembered—commissars often refer to themselves as first mates. The idea is similar to calling garbage collectors "sanitation engineers".

"Welcome to *Orekhova*, Dasha. I show you to cabin. Please—this way." Mikhail motioned for me to step in front of him. Smiling warmly at the other three men, I headed toward the living quarters of the ship. I greeted other crew members standing nearby and noticed that two men had picked up my baskets and duffel and followed along with us.

Approaching the hatchway, I instinctively bent over. Pausing on the threshold, I looked up and saw that head clearance was a good two feet. Even the doorway itself seemed wider than those on the Japanese boats. I stepped into the corridor and that unique fishing boat odor assaulted me. I breathed in the scent of unwashed bodies and fish; the aroma also told me that the toilet had to be nearby. A different smell from that of my Japanese ships, but it would become the defining one on all of my Soviet vessels. We trooped along on dirty green linoleum floors. Wooden hand railings lined the sickly green walls. Light bulbs in bare sockets dotted the ceiling at sporadic intervals. We passed by closed metal cabin doors with Russian words painted in red on them.

"Here, Dasha." The commissar stopped in front of an open door. "Your cabin." He grandly swept in front of me into the room. The two men with my gear stepped inside as well. One dropped the duffel and the other grinned at me. "Factory?" He pointed to the baskets. I nodded and said "*Spaciba,*" (thank you) and he trundled off.

The commissar said something in Russian to the duffel-carrier, and he smiled crookedly at me, clapping me on the back before he ducked out.

I surveyed my cabin. It was spacious and white, with a porthole looking out to sea. A large photograph of Lenin hung in one corner wall, his authoritarian stare bathing the room. Music whispered from a speaker box mounted next to him. Beside the box, a wall clock displayed the same time as my wristwatch. Perhaps tracking time on this ship would not be as difficult as on the *Kyowa*. A padded couch sat like a large steamer trunk, running the length of the wall beneath the porthole. In front of the couch, a small table was bolted to the forward wall. Unlike the forward-to-aft bunk layout on my Japanese boats, the bunks in this cabin ran port-to-starboard, one on top of the other. A large armoire loomed across from the bunks and beside it, a porcelain sink splashed with rust stains. Above it hung a mirror with no frame whose jagged edges would give Stephen King pause. Sunlight streamed through the open porthole, making the room seem light and airy. So much space, after my tiny cabin on the *Kyowa*, was a luxury. The window alone was enough to keep me content.

"Will be fine for you, Dasha?" The commissar eyed me questioningly.

"Oh, perfect, thank you." I nodded.

"Good. Now I show you other areas. Please follow me." The commissar led the way out of my room, first showing me how to lock the door and watching closely as I pocketed the key. I wondered why I would need to lock my door. To keep him out? I knew he must have his own keys to every area of the ship.

The commissar pointed out the cabins of the second mate, the factory manager, trawl master and the radio officer. He noted that the radio officer was a new arrival on the ship. I smiled grimly to myself. As we turned a corner, I knew from the smell that the next stop would be the toilet. Sure enough, Mikhail opened a door and proved me correct. I caught only a glimpse of an overhanging bare bulb and a brown bidet-toilet before Mikhail pulled the door shut and hurried me next door. As we stepped into the shower room, high school gym class came flooding back to me. I breathed in the smell of the locker room, eyeing the black streaks of mildew on the faded yellow paint. Torn rubber matting crisscrossed the floor. A soggy wooden bench sat in one corner, looking as if it might collapse at any moment. Four metal hooks sprouted from the wall above the bench. A rusty showerhead hung above two water spigots, one of which was bright red.

"We have baths every ten days. That is when engineer makes hot water. Also this is time we do all ship washing, when engineer make hot water. But, please, you may ask anytime for hot water for bath. Anytime, please." Mikhail nodded earnestly at me.

"Now please we go to captain's cabin for little party. Follow me, please." The commissar started up a set of stairs we had come to.

"But what about the factory? And the bridge? I need to see those areas, please." I wanted to get my work station established as soon as possible because I knew that, this being a joint venture fishery, the boat could receive a net very soon. We were already on the fishing grounds.

"Later, later." The commissar waved his hand dismissively. "Now party."

I tried to ignore the niggling concern in the back of my mind and followed the commissar up the stairs to the next level, which was one story above the deck level. Above this would be the bridge. So this boat had three levels above deck, not two as had the *Kyowa*.

The commissar opened a door and motioned me to precede him. I stepped into the captain's cabin and gasped at the banquet laid out before me. Dish after dish of pickles, onions, relishes, bread, meat, salads, cookies and beautifully decorated cakes covered the table in the center of the room. Five people sat surrounding this feast, and I recognized the captain, factory manager and chief mate. A woman with shoulder length black hair streaked with gray sat beside the chief mate. She smiled at me and said "My name Galena—ship doctor." The man beside her introduced himself as the radio officer.

"Dasha, Dasha, *sadis*." The captain eagerly patted the chair beside him, grinning hugely.

As I slipped into my seat, I picked up one of several green bottles in front of my plate and tried to read the label. The indecipherable Cyrillic alphabet stared back at me. Three blue volcanoes, set amidst craggy mountain splendor, outlined the writing.

"Like Alaska!" I tapped the label, showing it to the captain.

"Ah, yes. This mineral water is best in world. It is from area like Alaska—Kamchatka, very near to here. Special factory collects water from clear springs. All Kamchatka boats have this bottles of water." He beamed proudly.

"A toast." The commissar held up his glass. "To welcome Dasha to *Orekhova*." We all raised our glasses. "*Nasdarovia*—to your health."

The captain heaped piles of food onto my plate. Salted fish and pickles startled my taste buds. Sharp, vinegary salad made my eyes water. I rolled caviar eggs around on my tongue, enjoying their salty, briny taste before they melted away like butter. At home, caviar was such a luxury item that I never had occasion to eat it. Here, I would learn that it is a staple of the Soviet diet. Sturgeon caviar from the Black Sea—large black fish eggs on slices of hearty buttered bread—came to be one of my favorite delicacies on the *Orekhova* and all the ships that followed.

A slim woman with blonde shoulder length hair who reminded me of Meryl Streep slipped in and out of the room, removing plates and adding dishes of food. She introduced herself as Tatiana, the *bufetchitsa*. I learned that Tatiana was the captain's personal waitress, and she also served in the officers' dining room, where it was expected that I would have my meals. Later rumors told me that she was forced to serve as more than just a waitress to the captain.

Within an hour or so, the commissar said something in Russian to Tatiana, seeming to dismiss her. When she left the room, he locked the cabin door. The captain unlocked a massive armoire that sat against the wall, opening the door to reveal a phonograph player and cassette deck. He put on a lively Russian tape, deliberately turning the volume up high. He then opened a bottom drawer and pulled out three bottles of vodka, plunking them down onto the table. The commissar filled glasses all around; I tried to decline, but he would have none of it. Galena offered another toast, and I watched in amazement as everyone at the table swallowed the entire contents of their glass—and then repeated the ritual again . . . and again . . . and again. Both the captain and the chief mate urged me to drink more—to be polite I had sipped my vodka when joining in the toasts, but I just couldn't down it all. They kept trying to refill my glass and fussing when I didn't empty it. I felt awkward. I didn't want to insult my hosts by not drinking with them, but I simply could not handle the potent vodka whose few sips had burned like fire in my throat.

I wondered about Gorbachev's "dry boat" policy, which obviously was not adhered to in this room. I also wondered about the secrecy with which this group engaged in their drinking. I put on my innocent face and asked the commissar if everyone on the

Orekhova was free to drink alcohol. The commissar frowned and said this could not be allowed.

"Only officers can drink alcohol because it is against rules to drink. We drink because we are officers. But all others are too much like children to be allowed alcohol." His face red, the commissar sloshed more vodka toward my already full glass. Most of it ended up soaking my sweatshirt. He did not notice, elbowing Fyodor aside to offer me more caviar.

The party proceeded. Fyodor slumped sideways in his chair. The captain dribbled salad down his shirtfront. Galena and the radio officer fed each other caviar, the black eggs dropping from Galena's long pink tongue onto the table. Every time I tried to excuse myself, the captain clamped his hand on my arm and breathed fumes in my face.

"No, Dasha, you must not leave now. Party is only beginning!"

Finally he was too drunk to care, and I managed to slide out of my chair and out the door. I found the stairs down to the deck level where my cabin was, first making my way to the toilet. Though I could not remember its exact location, my nose lead me to the right door. Holding my breath, I opened the door and tiptoed across the urine-soaked floor to the toilet. The toilet itself was shaped like a large bidet, with no seat on it. Crusty human excrement covered its surface, and beside it sat a metal bucket filled with scraps of newspaper that had been used for wiping. Folded copies of *Pravda*, the state-run newspaper, were wedged into the roll bar attached to the wall beside the toilet. I made a mental note to keep a wad of toilet paper stuffed in my pocket at all times. Thanks to NMFS for encouraging me to bring my own. They had also warned me that, on Soviet ships, human waste was piped, untreated, directly into the sea. Trying not to feel guilty about this, I straddled the toilet, balancing delicately in order not to touch the filthy surface and gripping the roll bar tightly so I would not slide onto the slimy floor. I inhaled in short, shallow gasps to avoid being overwhelmed by the stench.

I returned to my cabin, flapping my clothes, trying to rid myself of the odor that seemed to cling to me.

A knock rattled my door. I opened it and a very tall blonde man stood smiling at me.

"*Dobry veicher*, Dasha. Second mate, Pyotr." His greeting was "Good Evening," now that it was dark outside. "Tapes?" He held out several cassette tapes.

"Come in, come in." I motioned him into the cabin and over to the padded bench beneath the porthole. I latched the door to the wall, hoping to get a cross breeze since the porthole was already open. I pulled out my small collection of tapes.

"What kind of music do you like?" I asked. Pyotr looked at me blankly. I imitated rock and roll music with drums and some raucous sounds, slower music by humming "Moon River."

"Heavy Metal! Aerosmith? Good American group, Aerosmith." Pyotr looked at me hopefully. Aerosmith—was that the band where the lead singer bit the heads off of bats? I wasn't sure. But heavy metal music was definitely not part of my collection.

I offered Pyotr a Talking Heads tape, which is as close as I could come to what he seemed to be interested in. He smiled broadly and insisted I take his tapes in exchange.

"Dasha, *spaciba*. My cabin—here." Pyotr motioned to the wall. He spoke in Russian, imitating knocking on his door if I needed anything. Another face appeared in my doorway. Pyotr and the new arrival exchanged quick, quiet words, and Pyotr pulled the man into the room, unlatching and shutting the door. Pyotr introduced him as Anatolig, the deck master. Pyotr indicated that he would be right back and ducked out.

Anatolig stood over six feet tall. Like a smooth porcelain bowl, his bald head shone above a fringe of soft brown hair. The corners of his brown mustache drooped, walrus-like, over his mouth, giving him a somber expression. His sorrowful look contrasted sharply with his dark eyes, which danced and sparkled. I was charmed. Dark green cotton coveralls sagged on Anatolig's large frame. He had tied a piece of frayed brown rope around his waist in an attempt to make them fit. This is the outfit I would see him in nearly every day. Tolig, as he told me to call him, was to become my best friend on the *Orekhova*.

Pyotr stepped into the cabin with bottles of mineral water and more cassette tapes. He pulled the door shut behind him, and we all sat down to have our own little party. I had a small tape player, and we put on one of his Russian tapes.

"Dasha, you have pictures?" Tolig inquired, pulling some of his own from a front pocket. He showed me a black-and-white photograph of a cherubic young woman with chubby cheeks smiling into the camera. "My wife, Marina." He smacked the picture with his lips. "Soon we have baby. Our number one. You have baby?"

I laughed and said no to the baby. I showed Tolig and Pytor pictures of my family and my good friends, as well as shots of North Carolina and Seattle.

Pyotr's home was in Ukraine and Tolig's in Russia. As he exchanged the Russian tape now playing for one of my country ones, Pyotr told me that he lived with his mother and two sisters in Kiev. We all listened for a few minutes to the twangy tape, until Pyotr's grimace indicated how he felt about the music.

"Dasha, what is this music? Very bad, I think. Like cats making—what is that?—YEOWWW!" He spoke in Russian to Tolig and we all laughed together.

Tolig picked up my small knapsack as if it belonged to him and unzipped the top. Later I would understand that the Soviets have no sense of personal property, since everything, from their homes to their carry bags, is subject to search by the state.

He extracted my stack of magazines, his eyes wide, and he and Pyotr fell on them like starving animals. Slowly they turned the pages of *People*, exclaiming in Russian. Tolig traced his finger down the line of a silver dress on a sleek runway model. Pyotr tapped a perfume advertisement, raising the magazine to his nose and sniffing.

Tolig pointed to a television set in the background of one photograph. "Dasha, how much this cost?"

Pyotr pushed him aside, waving an article on Japanese import cars, asking the same question.

Conversation ceased as the magazines consumed the men. They were like marathoners, gulping water at the end of a race.

"Tolig, Pyotr, please—take these magazines with you." It was 2 a.m. and I needed to sleep.

Startled, Tolig said "Oh, no, Dasha, we cannot have these magazines. Please, you must hide these. Maybe here." He stepped to my bunk and shoved the stack under the mattress.

No one seemed too concerned about fishing; I asked Tolig when the first net would come on. He shrugged and said he did not know.

He and Pyotr exchanged words in Russian. Pyotr opened the cabin door and peered out, looking both left and right. He motioned for Tolig to stay, and he stepped out, shutting the door behind him.

Tolig looked at me sheepishly. "Pyotr first make sure safe, then I go. No crew members allowed here. If caught . . ." He motioned a knife being drawn across his throat.

"Who?" I returned the knifing motion. "Why?"

"Of course commissar." Tolig shrugged. "This deck and above—officers only. Crew—below only."

Pyotr popped his head back in and said "*Pashli*—come." I imagined that the commissar and the rest of the officers were, by this time, too drunk to care what was going on. We said good night to each other.

I was exhausted from the company of the Soviets. Their attention and openness overwhelmed me, perhaps because I was so unused to it. The first days on my Japanese boats had always been quiet, and I was left alone unless I sought out company. Socializing came later, and never in personal cabins. Wearily, I slipped off my clothes. I slid under clean, crinkly sheets onto the bottom bunk. The mattress was firm but did not seem to be filled with sand. The pillow felt like a log under my ear. I knocked it around a bit, trying to make a place for my head with no luck. Scrambling through my duffel, I pulled out a soft wool sweater and folded it on top of the pillow. I sniffed the faint, familiar odor of my Japanese boats.

Despite my tiredness, questions, like ping pong balls, bounced in my head. Why couldn't Tolig borrow my magazines? And why should I hide them? I tried to imagine what it would be like to be unable to come and go as I pleased. I remembered curfews from my childhood. These regulations, of course, ended with adulthood. I wondered if the regular crew knew that the officers drank alcohol while they "were too much like children" to be allowed any. As I finally drifted off to sleep, the word *children* stood out in my jumbled thoughts.

TEN

Tea, Compot, and Spy Work

IN MY DREAM, THE UNBALANCED WASHING MACHINE THUMPED HEAVILY across the floor. I woke up, my hands tangled in the sheets, trying to turn off the annoying machine. The door to my cabin flew open and the commissar stepped over the threshold, unfazed by the fact that I was still in bed. Instead of apologizing as I expected, he greeted me with *"Dobre outrom."* Good morning.

"Dasha, breakfast is in 30 minutes. Please come to the officers' dining room then." He smiled crookedly down at me as I lay in my bunk.

Squinting at my watch, I saw that it was 7 a.m. I thanked him and waited for him to leave before jumping out of bed.

I turned the tap over the stained sink, my face reflected in the Stephen King mirror. Brown water trickled out, then stopped. Gurgling sounds emanated from the pipes that lead from the ceiling to the tap. The gurgling turned to clanking and the pipes began to shake. I watched as they twitched and groaned. Fearing an explosion, I jumped back from the sink just as the trickle turned into a gush of rusty water. The flow spewed over the edge of the sink and soaked my T-shirt, even though I stood a few feet away. The NMFS warning not to drink the water on Soviet ships appeared to have been an understatement.

I pulled on the clothes I had worn the day before, baggy blue jeans and a heavy plaid work shirt. Stuffing tissue into my pocket, I steeled myself and left my cabin for that delightful spot, the toilet room. This morning the smoke of cigarettes mingled with the urine and excrement smell. The used paper bin overflowed with crumpled and soiled pages of *Pravda*. The sloshing water on the floor almost crested the tops of my Birkenstocks. Perhaps I would start wearing my boots to the bathroom.

Returning to my cabin, I dared to turn the tap again. This time, a pale brown geyser shot from the faucet. As if in hopes of offsetting the rusty tap water, a bar of strong industrial soap sat in the small holder beside the sink. I used it to wash my hands thoroughly, savoring its strong antiseptic smell after the aromatic nightmare of moments ago.

At 7:30 a.m., as I entered the officers' dining room, clock chimes like those of Big Ben sounded from the speaker box perched in the corner. A man's voice spoke in rapid Russian. The galley was located at the bow of the ship, and portholes dotted the front wall of the room through which bright sunshine streamed in. A long padded bench sat below these windows, behind a wooden table covered with a white tablecloth. Four high-backed chairs lined the side of the table nearest me, with two more at each end. Beside the crackling speaker box and clock, the stern countenance of Lenin contrasted with the dancing sunbeams. The commissar perched on one end of the bench; beside him was the factory manager, then the radio officer. I recognized the back of the chief mate, who turned and patted the seat to his right, winking as he caught my eye. The head chair, which I assumed belonged to the captain, was empty. Each of the men nodded and said, *"Dobry outrom."*

I slipped into my assigned seat. An intricately folded white swan graced my delicate china plate. I hated to shake it out into a plain linen napkin. A grandmotherly porcelain teapot sat in the middle of the table. Beside it, a dented metal pitcher. I watched the commissar pour first from the china pot—half a cup of strong, black tea. Then, from the dented metal pot, half a cup of hot water to cut the strength of the tea. I went next, adding milk and sugar to my tea from the delicate china containers. The men did the same, except that they each dumped at least three teaspoons of sugar in their cups of tea. I thought no one, anywhere in the world, could top my sugar consumption—until I started working on Soviet ships. These men had a fondness for the sweet white powder that even I could not approach.

Tatiana entered and placed steaming bowls of white porridge in front of us. Next she brought out a basket of warm brown bread. I looked over my shoulder and saw an area off of the dining room that appeared to be her serving space. A sink and small stove filled the tiny room, but it was not a fully equipped kitchen. The main galley and crew's mess were one deck below, on my level. The commissar had not included these on our tour. To serve us, Tatiana carried her plates and bowls of food up the stairs at every meal. I thanked her, and she smiled warmly at me.

Each man said "*Pretna appetitia*" before he began eating, and I did the same. The porridge, swimming in butter, was smooth and salty, a cross between grits and Cream of Wheat. Hefting a slab of the hearty bread onto my plate, I reached for the butter dish next to the basket. I sank my knife into the soft, pale yellow butter and spread it onto my bread. This was almost as good as the caviar.

I turned to the chief mate. "Sasha, when will we pick up our first net?"

Waving his bread, he replied, "I think sometime this afternoon. Maybe 1600 hours." He winked at me yet again.

The commissar spoke up. "Dasha, I will show you factory after lunch."

Politely, I replied, "I must go very soon—after breakfast. I need to set up my work station. I also need to see the bridge."

Frowning, the commissar said something to Fyodr, the factory manager, in Russian. "Dasha, Fyodr Pyotrovitch shall show you factory. I myself have much business to attend to so cannot be free for you."

Upon finishing his breakfast, each man stood and said again, "*Pretna appetitia*" before leaving the table. The commissar told me breakfast was 7:30, lunch was 11:30 and supper was served at 5:30 p.m. I asked what happened if I had to miss a meal because I was working.

"Oh, maybe you finish work by mealtimes. I think is no

problem. Last observer always eat." He shrugged. "Fyodr say factory tour in 15 minutes. He come to your cabin."

Thanking the commissar, I said, *"Pretna appetitia"* and left the dining room. Returning to my cabin, I pulled out my raingear and boots, plastic forms and other paraphernalia I needed to take to the factory. I assumed my baskets were already there, trusting that the crew member of yesterday had taken them down.

Fifteen minutes passed. Then 30. Then 45. Giving up on Fyodr, I decided to poke around myself. My curiosity urged a search for the crew's mess. I knew it was somewhere on my level. It was interesting that the commissar had not shown it to me. I guessed that it was probably on the opposite side from where my cabin was located. Grabbing my gear, I headed in that direction. The living quarters were laid out in a large upside-down U shape, with the bottom of the U leading out onto the trawl deck. My cabin was on the port side of the U and, sure enough, the crew's mess was on the starboard side of the U, directly opposite my cabin. Men sauntered in and out of the mess as I strode up to the door, and several of them stopped and greeted me.

"Hello, Dasha! Welcome, Dasha!" I was dazed by their warmth and friendliness. "Please, come in." Two of the men urged me forward and into the mess.

Divided by a partition, a lounging area took up part of the large space. The dining side, on the far side of the divider, contained five rows of wooden tables with wooden benches in front of each. The lounge area, where I now stood, looked like a casual living room, furnished with Goodwill bargain pieces. Wood-framed chairs with faded yellow and green coverings sprawled about, a couple of them tipped on their backs. Like props from an old southern mansion, two shabby upholstered chairs took center stage, tufts of stuffing masquerading as buds among the wilting roses of the material. Scarred from years of abuse by heavy fishing boots, three wooden coffee tables angled crazily in front of the chairs. Copies of *Pravda* and dog-eared Russian paperback books lay on their dull surfaces. I thought of my poor-student college days, when we would scavenge the town dump and drag home odd bits of furniture to display proudly, if haphazardly, in our communal living area. The room, of course, would not be complete without the requisite picture of Lenin; he hung in his usual position on the wall beside the clock and speaker box.

We crossed to the rows of tables, and the men sat me down on the hard wooden bench. They marched to the serving counter, where they dipped a battered ladle into a large enamel pot, filling dented metal mugs. Beyond them was the galley itself. From ceiling hooks, huge pots and pans swung gently in time with the rolling of the ship. A woman tended several pots on the stovetop, her large white chef's hat drooping from the steam like a soggy doughnut on top of her head. I recognized her from my arrival on deck yesterday. She smiled and waved at me, knocking askew her limp pastry headdress as she wiped her face. Behind the woman, a man worked in front of a tall oven, pulling out loaves of hot brown bread and placing them on the floury counter beside him. His white chef's hat puffed out nicely, like a spinnaker under full beam.

"*Dobry dzien*, Dasha." Several men plopped onto the hard wooden bench, with big smiles and lots of metal teeth all around. One man took the lead, introducing himself as Sasha and going around the now crowded table: Fyodr, Alexi, Mikhail, Valerya, Achmed, Igor, and Dimitri. Just then, my two friends from the serving counter returned, and they set a metal mug in front of me.

"*Peet, Peet,* Dasha. Compot." The men urged me to "drink, drink" as they sat down and did so.

Grape Kool Aid mixed with thick, sweet syrup slid down my throat. Surely the Soviets would not have anything as imperialistically American as Kool Aid on board—what was this stuff? Sasha told me that the cooks boiled fruit, then skimmed off the flavored water and add massive amounts of sugar. Compot, like caviar, was a staple aboard every Soviet ship on which I worked.

An ethnic sampling of the Soviet Union surrounded me. Alexi and Mikhail, from Russia, had traditional Slavic faces, with high cheekbones and fair features. Achmed, with his dark skin and jet black hair, contrasted sharply with these two. Before landing on the *Orekhova*, Achmed had spent his days high up in the mountains of Azerbaijan, tending his family's herd of goats. He frightened me, somehow, with his smoldering good looks and black-eyed intense gaze. Igor was from Kazakhstan and Valerya, Ukraine. Dimitri was Asian and much smaller than his companions. His North Korean parents had lived in Russia for many years. Not far from home, Fyodr lived in Kamchatka, the peninsula across the Bering Sea from Alaska where the Soviet mineral water came from.

I heard my name being called from the doorway of the mess hall. I looked to see Tolig striding toward me, waving, a bright smile on his face.

"*Dobry outrom*, Dasha!" Tolig greeted me with "Good morning." The other men moved over, making room for him to sit beside me. I felt a connection with Tolig, after our time together last evening.

"Tolig, can you show me factory?" I questioned him.

"Factory? No problem. Now?" He stood back up. I gathered up my gear and moved to go with him. There was a commotion among the men. Tolig spoke to them and turned to me, saying that they wanted me to come back and talk with them when I finished touring the factory. I thanked the men, and we moved toward the door. Tolig whistled across the room at another group of men; one of them detached himself and came over to us. Like Achmed, he also had Arabic features and a short, black crew cut. His height matched mine. He stuck out his hand, grinning.

"Dasha, he is Reshat, member of my trawl crew." Tolig introduced us. I pumped Reshat's hand, smiling back at him. The two conferred in Russian, then the three of us left the mess hall. I followed Tolig and Reshat as we turned right. Bright sunlight streamed into the dim corridor through the open entryway door. We stepped through it onto the warm deck. What a difference from my winter time cruises.

The worn wooden deck of the *Orekhova* contrasted sharply with the slippery metal one of the *Kyowa*. Unlike the Japanese boat, where everything had been neatly arranged, there seemed to be no order on the trawl deck of the *Orekhova*. Nets sprawled haphazardly in different areas. Dozens of rusty barrels lined the railings, and tarnished buoys and weights created a junk yard effect.

I expected to see old engines and perhaps a carburetor or muffler. Picking my way carefully through the clutter, I noticed, flying proudly from the stern, the large Soviet flag—bright red with the gold hammer and sickle glistening in the sun.

We walked all the way to the stern of the ship along the starboard side. Tolig stopped in front of a rusty, dented three-sided bin, the fourth wall being the actual side of the boat. A matching bin was positioned on the port side of the deck. The thin metal walls reached my neck.

"*Riba* here." Tolig patted the side of the bin. So these were the two fish-holding bins—above deck, unlike the below-deck ones on the *Kyowa*.

I pulled my tape measure out of my pocket and piled my other gear down on the deck. I told Tolig that I needed to get inside the fish bin to measure it and imitated climbing into the bin, waving my tape measure to demonstrate. Both he and Reshat exchanged puzzled looks, and Tolig said, "You go *in* there, Dasha?"

I nodded and looked around for something to stand on. Reshat poked Tolig, and they both knelt in front of me, crossing their hands, prepared to boost me up. I protested that I would hurt them, but they insisted that I climb onto the makeshift hoist of their clasped hands. As gently as I could, I stepped onto their hands and they stood up, lifting me into the air until I was waist high with the top of the wall. Bracing my hands on the side of the fish bin for balance, I swung one leg over the edge and then the other. The wall bent slightly under my weight. There was nowhere to sit on its pencil thin metal edge, so I fell over sideways and landed heavily on the wooden deck.

"Dasha! Dasha!" Unintelligible words of Russian. I looked up to see both Reshat and Tolig staring down at me, their eyes wide.

I laughed up at them and waved away their concern, quickly getting to my feet. I would probably have a bruised thigh to show for this, but that was all.

My tape measure had landed in the far corner of the bin, so I retrieved it and motioned for Tolig to find one of my plastic forms. Amazingly, my pencil remained clipped to the pocket of my shirt.

I heard the men scrabbling around in my gear pile, and Tolig handed two plastic forms over the top into my waiting hands.

A bell sounded on the deck and someone called Tolig's name from the bridge. He shouted back and forth with an unseen figure and then turned to me.

"Excuse please, Dasha. Back soon." Tolig grabbed Reshat's sleeve and the two trotted off together.

I measured the sides of the bin, both up and down and length wise. I estimated that it would hold about five tons of fish, similar to the *Kyowa*'s capacity. Finished with my measurements, I sat down to await the return of Tolig and Reshat.

Ten minutes passed. Then 15. After 30 minutes, I decided not to take personally the fact that I had been abandoned, forgotten in a fish bin. Now what was I going to do? I stared at the smooth sides of the bin. Gripping the top, I tried to heave myself up with no success. That sure-to-defeat-me pull up contest again. I looked up to the bridge but could see nothing through the glass window. There was no one anywhere on deck.

"Dasha! Dasha!" Relieved, I heard Tolig's shout and saw him and Reshat running toward me from the living quarters.

They arrived, breathless, at the fish bin and grinned at me over the wall. Again, I gripped the top of the bin. Tolig and Reshat leaned over the wall. Each of them grabbed the waistband of my blue jeans and, with a combination of pulling and tugging, heaved me headfirst over the side of the bin, the three of us tumbling to the deck. I landed on top, my face in Tolig's crotch, one hand on Reshat's thigh. I rolled around, trying to release the men beneath me, but, like octopus tentacles, we only became more entangled. Finally we managed to separate, and I sat up, gasping. Tolig's face blushed bright red and Reshat's eyes streamed with tears. We staggered to our feet, and I leaned against that troublesome fish bin, bent double laughing. Finally recovered, the men led the way toward the factory.

Reshat opened a hatchway door, and we descended a short flight of steps, leaving the bright sun behind. Ahhh! That familiar aroma of fish immediately surrounded me. The observer's perfume . . .

A maze of rusty conveyor belts and a slimy floor greeted me. I felt the ceiling pressing down. It was filled with large hanging pipes that seemed to pull it even lower. I had some sense of the fish flow and wandered among the battered machinery, carefully watching for the pipes above my head, which was a trick with the dim lighting. A few functioning bare light bulbs glowed weakly from random spots on the ceiling. Cracked and jagged bulbs menaced me from the remaining sockets.

The factory lay out differed slightly from the *Kyowa's*, but the idea was the same. I spotted my baskets near the mouth of the fish bin, at a work station established by the previous observer. I tossed my gear here, mentally reviewing the things I needed to do to get set up.

We continued our tour, Tolig showing me the flash freezers and the below deck freezer hold.

Suddenly, Tolig snapped his fingers and said, "*Mookar!*" He and Reshat turned and headed back toward the stern of the ship, where we had first entered. Trotting along, I mentally reviewed the Russian vocabulary sheet that NMFS had given me, puzzling over the word *mookar*. We arrived at what looked like a trap door built into the floor, tucked behind the stairway that led up to the trawl deck. Tolig bent over and yanked on the two solid metal handles on the door. The door squeaked open; it was hinged and folded back onto the floor. Tolig turned, and stepping backwards down some ladder like stairs, disappeared into the darkness below. Reshat, who was behind me, motioned for me to follow. I wondered wildly if *mookar* meant below-deck prison. I had fleeting visions of landing in a pit full of men chained to the walls. Pirates, maybe. Certainly they would have no teeth, a few would be missing limbs. They would be emaciated and near death, but they would have enough life left to shake their chains at my arrival.

Reshat gently prodded me forward. As I stepped downward, I smelled an odor unlike the one to which I had become accustomed.

It seemed a combination of sour milk, manure and fish food. The gloomy air danced with dust and, as my eyes adjusted, I saw dozens of bulky burlap sacks stacked one on top of the other, all around the walls. I heard no rattling chains and saw no toothless men. A large piece of equipment loomed in the corner, shaped like a kitchen oven, but five times the normal size. We walked over to it, and I saw a funnel running from the top of the machine back up to the factory. Perhaps this was the passageway to allow air into the machine and the men were imprisoned inside it. Tolig swung open the heavy metal front door and motioned for me to reach inside. I peered in and saw what looked like sawdust heaped on the bottom. A relief, no shackled men. The sour milk-and-manure smell enveloped me. Reaching down, I touched a soft, powdery material. Forget the prison, perhaps this was a secret cocaine storage. I grabbed a handful of the stuff and lifted it out into the gloomy light. Puzzled, I looked questioningly at Tolig and Reshat.

"Fish grinder, Dasha. Big fish, now little pieces—*mookar*." Tolig said. Of course—this was fish meal and this whole area the fish meal plant. Now all the strange equipment made sense, as did the unusual smell.

After we climbed out of the below-deck prison/fish meal plant, I asked Tolig where Fyodr, the factory manager was, trying to explain that he had been scheduled to show me around but had never shown up. At the mention of Fyodr, both Tolig and Reshat rolled their eyes at each other and laughed.

"*Lintai, lintai.*" Tolig said. I later translated this as "lazy," and it would prove true of Fyodr, at least as far as actual fishing work was concerned. Very rarely was I to see him in the factory. It seemed that Fyodr's job was more to work with the commissar on the political mission of keeping the crew in line than to oversee the activities of the factory.

We completed our tour and Tolig said he now wanted to show me "most important" area. I followed him through the factory, and we emerged into a dark, dingy corridor that smelled strongly of unwashed bodies, cigarette smoke and sickly sweet cologne. The crew's living quarters. I heard loud laughter from one of the cabins lining the corridor, and several men popped out of various doorways, exchanging words with their neighbors. A few of the men saw me, and immediately greeted me. "Dasha! Dasha! *Dobre outre!*" Hearing this, men, it seemed, poured out of nearly every cabin, waving and calling my name. Several beckoned me to come to their cabin, saying, "*Chi!* Dasha, *Chi!*" I knew this meant they wanted me to join them for tea. But Tolig spoke to a couple of the men and then hurried up some stairs back to the deck. Reshat and I followed him. We came out onto the port side of the deck and ducked into a small room built along the side of the boat.

"Here, Dasha—chi room. When no work, we stay here, drink chi, talk." Tolig swept his arm around the room. A waist-high counter ran the length of the wall. Two portholes let in light. Overturned crates, obviously make-shift chairs, crowded the space. A frayed electrical cord wound its way, snake-like, across the counter and connected with an iron hot plate. A second frayed cord hung over the edge of the counter. My eyes followed it to a dangerous looking electric teapot. I supposed the Soviets didn't have an OSHA equivalent in the USSR. Battered metal mugs, two bags of sugar and several dented cans of condensed milk were arranged beside the teapot.

"*Pezalsta, sadis.*" Tolig motioned for me to sit down, and Reshat pulled a crate up for me. Tolig busied himself with tea preparation. Suddenly, two heads appeared in the doorway—Alexi and Mikhail, who had befriended me earlier in the crew's mess. Reshat beckoned, and they pulled the hatch door shut behind them as they stepped quickly in to join us. Tolig looked over his shoulder, saying something to Reshat, who locked the door. Alexi and Mikhail drew up crates and sat down.

"Together we work." Oleg pointed to the three men and himself.

"Only four?" I inquired.

"Oh, one more—also Sasha." I had, it seemed, already met a dozen Sashas, so I assumed I would soon find out which one was the fifth member of this trawl crew.

Tolig stepped over from the tea area and handed me a steaming mug of tea, heavily sweetened with condensed milk. The other men took turns fixing their own mugs of tea. I stiffened as the door latch rattled. Tolig put his finger to his lips. It rattled again, then whoever was on the other side walked heavily away.

"Who?" I looked questioningly at Tolig. "Why did you lock the door?"

"Ah, Dasha." Tolig shook his head wearily. "On this boat, many spuins—spies. Commissar is very bad man who makes trouble. Spuins tell commissar who talks to observer. So we must to be careful."

The four men exchanged words in Russian, and Reshat and Tolig both laughed at something Alexi said. I asked Tolig who the spies were.

"*Lintai* Fyodr, factory manager." The men all laughed again.

"What about *starpom,* the chief mate?"

I was relieved when Tolig replied, "Oh, no, *starpom* is good man."

The four men rattled off several other names of "spuins" but I couldn't place faces with them. However, it would soon become apparent who these men were, as they were ostracized by the rest of the crew and especially by this trawl crew.

The five of us drank tea, laughed and teased each other. Reshat pulled a small pin from his pocket and gave it to me. Its design of three volcanoes was silver, blue and green. In tiny Cyrillic letters, the word "Kamchatka" glistened at me. Beside me, Reshat pulled at my sleeve and then hunkered down low on his crate, his arms pulled over his tucked head. Suddenly, he shot upward, bellowing "KA-POW!!" and throwing his arms toward the ceiling. Startled, I fell backwards off my crate, dropping my tea mug onto the floor. Surrounded by guffawing men, I stumbled to my feet.

"Dasha, Reshat, he is to be volcano—like on your pin." Thank goodness—I thought he was having some sort of fit. Tolig continued, "In Kamchatka are many volcanoes, same like Alaska, I think."

Alexi placed another small pin in my hands, a red one with a gold spaceship in the middle. Again, Reshat crouched low, this time on the floor, and blasted off with appropriate sound effects. I gathered there was some concern on his part that, as with the volcanoes, I might not know what a spaceship was.

The talk turned to business, and I learned that there were two trawl crews of five men each. Each crew worked eight hour shifts. The other trawl chief—Tolig's counterpart—was the man who had picked me up from the *Excalibur* in the lifeboat.

"He is Oleg. Good man, Dasha." Tolig said.

The crews were responsible for landing the nets on deck when they were delivered by the catcher boats and emptying them into the fish bins. If the *Orekhova* had been trawling on her own and not operating as a joint venture, the deck crew would have worked only on deck, setting and pulling in the nets. In the joint venture fishery, the crew had only to retrieve nets from the catcher boats, leaving them with lots of extra time. This "extra time" was to be put to use in the factory—it was expected that the crew work on the processing line once they were finished on deck.

When this topic came up, there was a good deal of grumbling among the men. No one, it seemed, wanted to work in the factory.

"Only low men work down there. On deck, high men. We are big men," Tolig spread his hands "Down there, little men."

Tolig asked me what time it was, and I looked at my watch: 11:45. He jumped to his feet.

"Dasha—lunch now. You must go or commissar search for you." I wondered if I would have to worry about pleasing the commissar the entire cruise. I thanked the men, waving good-bye, and headed off to the officers' dining room.

Tatiana greeted me happily when I arrived, and both the chief mate and commissar bade me sit down. We were the only three at the table. Saying "*Pretna appetita*," I dipped my spoon into the bowl of beet borscht, dotted with sour cream, that sat before me. The borscht slid down my throat with a delicious sweetness.

"Sasha, after eating, may I come and look at the bridge, please?" I asked the chief mate. He and the commissar exchanged words, and the commissar said that Sasha would be happy to guide me around the bridge after lunch. He asked me if I had learned everything about the factory that I needed to.

"Yes, thank you." I decided not to mention the fact that Fyodr had never shown up.

"Tolig knows much about deck and factory. I am glad he assist you." My God, this man did know everyone's whereabouts. "Dasha, if you want any compot or tea, you may ask Tatiana to get for you. No need to go to crew area." He smiled smoothly at me.

I nodded politely, glad to see Tatiana as she brought our main course. She removed my soup bowl and set in front of me a plate heaped with a grain dish that I identified as bulgur. And—I blinked my eyes—a pink, stubby tongue lay thickly beside the bulgur. I glanced at both the commissar and chief mate as they cut into their tongues with relish. I had a fleeting thought that perhaps these were the tongues of crew members who had talked too freely with the observer or committed some other transgression. Then I decided that they were probably just lamb tongues. Cutting into my tongue delicately, I placed a small piece in my mouth and chewed hesitantly. Hmm . . . not a bad taste. But not as good as the caviar.

Finishing, the commissar excused himself. Within a few minutes, Sasha and I completed our meals and left the dining room together to go to the bridge. As I left, I waved and thanked Tatiana, who smiled at me.

Just outside the officers' mess, the chief mate and I walked by a door that stood slightly ajar. Through it I glimpsed the commissar bent over some kind of reel-to-reel tape equipment. Having been tipped off by the deck crew that Sasha was OK, I tapped him on the shoulder, pointing to this scene.

"What is he doing?" I whispered. A finger on his lips, Sasha motioned me forward, pulling me through the doorway and onto the stairs leading to the bridge. Rolling his eyes, he whispered in my ear "Commissar doing spy work. Very important." He winked.

We climbed the few steps to the bridge. I gasped in surprise at the big, open space. What a contrast to the compact, cluttered bridge of the *Kyowa*. Large, salt-scummed windows surrounded the bridge on all four sides. Through the stern window, I gazed down on the entire trawl deck.

Padded benches claimed space on both the port and starboard walls, with large, empty tables in front of them. Metal bolts held the loran unit and some other pieces of equipment into the starboard wall above the chart table. The VHF radio crackled and sputtered next to them. A chipped metal electric teapot with a familiar dangerous cord sat on the chart table like an accident waiting to happen. China cups clinked gently beside it. Brown tea stains mingled with reef markings on the charts.

On the port wall, above the stairway, Lenin's stern face gazed down, his eyes seeming to follow me everywhere as I moved around the bridge.

Pyotr, my neighbor and the second mate, greeted us from his post at the electronic steering wheel just in front of the bow window.

"*Dobre outrom*, Pyotr. You like the Talking Heads tape?" I wondered if he had listened to it yet.

"Oh, thank you Dasha. But that tape, it is too easy for me. You have no heavy metal?" Pyotr tried one more time.

I was sorry I had no heavy metal tapes to loan him. Perhaps if I had, his sad expression might lighten up.

Pyotr pointed out the *Orekhova's* fish finding unit, a throwback to Captain Bligh days. This unit did not have a monitor but actually printed out a black-and-white graph of the bottom of the sea and other formations that the sonar picked up. The heavier the black squiggly graph marks, the better the chance of a good school of fish.

I asked the chief mate to show me the Daily Cumulative Catch Log. He pulled out a sliding drawer below the chart table, filled with various logbooks. We flipped through the DCCL together, Sasha pointing out large catches and unusual species the ship had recorded.

Assuming I would see the captain on the bridge, I questioned the chief mate. "Sasha, where is the captain? I have not seen him anywhere this morning."

Sasha laughed and, circling his middle finger against his thumb, flicked the side of his neck. A sore throat? Sick?

"Sick . . . yes . . . from too much drink." Sasha again repeated the flicking motion against his neck, which I would see used regularly to indicate over-drinking. He and Pyotr laughed.

"When will we take a net of fish?" I questioned the chief mate. Sasha said something to Pyotr. He then turned to me and said that Pyotr had recently spoken with the nearest catcher boat, which now had a net in the water and hoped to deliver it around 1600 hours—4 p.m. It was 2 now, so I decided to go back to my cabin and organize my work materials in preparation for the net coming on.

Thanking both Sasha and Pyotr, I headed down the stairs to the officers' deck. I paused before the mysterious spy door and quietly peered around the door sill. The door had been pulled mostly shut, but it was still ajar. Through the crack, I glimpsed the commissar sitting in front of his recording equipment with headphones on, hunched over a yellow tablet, writing rapidly. I tiptoed quietly by, so as not to catch his attention and hurried back to my cabin.

ELEVEN

Hide and Seek

I HAD BEGUN CHECKING WITH THE BRIDGE AT 3 THAT AFTERNOON IN anticipation of the 4 p.m. trawl being brought on. At 6:45 p.m., the *Orekhova* finally began steaming to the spot where the *Miss Emily*, the catcher boat, reported that it held a net for pick up. I perched on the stool beside the stern window as the *Miss Emily* came into view. Round orange floats, attached to a bobbing black shape, bounced on the surface of the water like glistening Christmas tree ornaments.

The chief mate eased back on the *Orekhova*'s engines, and we glided toward the catcher boat. Tolig and the other deck crew members stood clustered at the stern ramp, and Tolig had a long iron hook slung across his shoulders. I spotted Mikhail at the winch controls. Like shiny yellow beacons, three Helly-Hansen clad crewmen waved from the small stern deck of the *Miss Emily*. Reshat and Alexi bent over an empty folded net attached to a cable and shoved it down the stern ramp, Mikhail playing out cable as the net slipped into the sea. The bouncing catcher boat angled toward the empty net, and one of the men reached over the side, hooking an end of the net with his pole and attaching it to a cable. The net crawled up the stern ramp like a caterpillar.

Tolig waved toward the bridge and the *Orekhova* reversed engines, moving slowly backward toward the net of fish. With finely tuned movements, the *Orekhova* pulled beside the drifting net and Tolig shimmied partway down the stern ramp. He leaned out and managed to hook the line that anchored the net to a marker buoy. Reshat danced beside him, his hands held over his head, clasping a taut cable. At a signal from Tolig, Reshat pushed the cable toward him and Tolig attached it to the line. Both men turned and pulled themselves back up the stern ramp. The winches whined and Mikhail began sliding the pod of fish up the stern ramp.

This net contained only about 10 tons of pollock. Pyotr, the second mate, had taken over the controls of the ship, and the chief mate now stood beside me, gazing down at the small catch as it rolled gently on the deck. He asked me what tonnages the *Kyowa* had brought on and was astounded when I told him 50-90, regularly. Fishing as a joint venture, the *Orekhova* was forced to accept nets of 10-15 tons because that was as much as the small catcher boats could manage at one time. I knew the *Orekhova* could process and hold several thousand tons of fish. I also knew that there were two factory crews of 9-10 people each—plus the additional help of the five members of each deck crew. I assumed that we would bring on nets frequently since the tonnages were so small. I was to learn differently. We may have had the labor force to process twice what we did on the *Kyowa*, but the work environment, atmosphere, and ethic was very different on this boat.

The chief mate and I watched the deck crew dump the glistening pollock into the two holding bins, and I rushed down to the chi room on deck to put on my rain gear. Worried about getting a late start, I raced to the factory hoping I had not missed too much of the first flow of fish.

I arrived to a silent and deserted factory. The doors to the fish bin had been left open, and fresh pollock streamed out onto the still conveyor belt. The fish thumped and twisted, flopping onto the floor. I shuffled my blue baskets and kicked around at my work station, waiting for the crew to show up. Finally I heard an announcement over the loudspeaker and, slowly, men began entering through the back of the factory, just off the crew's living quarters. Many had mugs of tea in their hands and none had on their work gear. I walked back to greet them. One of the men I had met in the crew's mess, Valodya, stepped forward and said, "*Dobre viecher*, Dasha! I am boss of this crew." The overall factory manager, Fyodr, was nowhere to be seen.

I plopped down on a conveyor belt as the men surrounded me. One of them held his ragged dull green rain jacket up beside my sparkling yellow outfit and rolled his eyes, saying something in Russian which caused everyone to laugh. I fingered the jacket. The rubber felt thin and soft. Even a semi-sharp object could easily poke through the weak material. The sleeves hung in tatters; the right one had been mended with clear fishing line. I looked at the jackets of the other men. Most had large patches and stitched tears.

Several of the men wrapped heavy rags around their thin socks before putting on their lightweight rubber boots. There were no steel-toed boots here. A couple of the men wandered ahead to the factory and began turning on conveyor belts and saws. Slowly the fish began to wend their way along the conveyor belt. Casually, the first line worker picked up a single pollock, sliding its head through the whirring saw. Yawning, he reached for another fish. The second man on the line lazily grabbed a couple of fish and shoved them through his saw. I had no trouble collecting my samples. The fish moved so slowly along the conveyor that it took me many minutes before I even filled my basket. I shook my head, remembering the frantic chaos and speed of the *Kyowa's* factory.

By midnight, we had finished our work. About four hours to process 10 tons of fish. I asked Valodya if we would bring on another net of fish soon and he told me not until tomorrow, probably mid-morning.

As I prepared to leave the factory, Tolig stuck his head through the deck door and looked down the stairs at me.

"Dasha! *Pashli!*" He motioned for me to come with him. I stumbled along behind him as he led me over the dark deck to the chi room. Tolig opened the door and waved me in. Reshat, Oleg, Kolia and Sasha all grinned at me, pulling a crate up for me to sit on. Tolig tugged the door shut behind him and, I noticed, did not lock it.

Tolig handed me a mug of tea, saying, "Dasha, tonight we make *kartoshka*—you like." I looked puzzled and, from under the counter, Reshat pulled out a bag of potatoes and held them up. "*Kartoshka!*" He grinned.

Oleg opened his jacket, pulling an evil-looking knife from the holder attached to his rope belt. Each of the others wore similar contraptions. They proudly showed me their knives, demonstrating how sharp they were on various surfaces. I nodded and gaped, thoroughly impressed and determined to remain on the good side of these fellows. Reshat grabbed a potato and deftly peeled it in one swift motion. He then cut the naked tuber into bite-size chunks. The other men began peeling potatoes as Tolig fired up the hot plate. I held the pot with the potato chunks and, after there was a sizable pile of peeled and chunked potatoes, Tolig fried them with butter in a medium-sized pan, liberally adding salt. He then carefully served up five metal plates of delicious potatoes.

Just as we were stacking our plates after finishing, without warning, the door flew open, and the commissar stepped into the chi room. There was silence as he surveyed the scene. "*Dobre viecher.*" He nodded at all of us. A couple of the men echoed his greeting, as I did. He said something to Tolig, who hunched his shoulders and followed him out of the room.

All I could think was that I had been on the *Orekhova* for only two days and already I had caused trouble for someone. Oleg spoke the best English, so I asked him if Tolig was in trouble. And what about the rest of them?

"The commissar, he is *kazul*. Maybe small problem for Tolig, I don't know. He tell us after." The men muttered among themselves; I caught the word "*kazul*" several times. I asked Oleg what it meant.

"*Kazul* is like a—what is word?—small animal with little beard. Makes sounds, 'Baaa! Baaaa!' It is big insult to call person this word."

A goat, I surmised. I would have to remember this word. I could tell there would be occasion to use it.

I gathered up my things and prepared to leave. Oleg motioned for me to wait, and he stepped out to check on where the commissar and Tolig were.

"Dasha, they stand beside near door into ship. Best for you to go to other side." Oleg held the door open for me. I quietly said good-bye to the other men and slipped out into the blackness.

Tolig and the commissar stood just a few yards away, illuminated by one of the spotlights that ringed the entry area. Tolig was facing me, and the commissar had his back to me. The look on Tolig's face was one of consternation. I stealthily cut across the darkened deck and headed to the starboard entry door. A spotlight also shone on this doorway, so I ducked my head as I hurried through the hatchway. I passed by the crew's mess and saw several men sitting around drinking tea.

"Dasha! *Sadis!*" They motioned for me to join them. I waved and continued down the corridor. Knowing the commissar was on the prowl, I thought it best to lie low. Rounding the corner, I reached my cabin and stepped inside, quickly shutting the door behind me. I leaned against it, my heart pounding. This didn't seem real. I felt like a kid again, playing hide and seek. I remembered the delicious thrill of hiding from my pursuer. The electric jolt of fear when I was discovered. The shrieks and laughter that followed. But this was not a game. This hide and seek was a way of life for the Soviets, not something they played at. Of all of the people on this ship, I knew that I was the only one to whom this felt like a game.

*   *   *

I saw Tolig mid-morning the next day. I went out on deck to the chi room to see if I could find him and instead found Reshat, who went down to the crew's cabins to get Tolig. I was not going to venture down there without knowing that it was safe to do so. Tolig appeared a few minutes later, smiling and happy to see me. I asked him about the incident with the commissar the night before, and he told me there was "little problem" between him and the commissar.

"Look, Tolig, I don't want to get you into trouble. You must tell me what is OK to do. Maybe I should not visit with y'all in the chi room?" I really did not want to make problems for these men.

"Oh, no, Dasha! Is only little problem. Not big problem. Please, you must drink tea with us. We miss you if you not come here!" Tolig's expression changed from earnest and eager to puzzled. "Dasha, what is this word you say—yarl?"

We proceeded to have a short lesson in Southern American English, until we both decided that Tolig would never pronounce "y'all" correctly.

"Dasha, Tatiana want you to come with her tonight to sauna. Maybe after work you go with her and other women crews. You will come?" Tolig asked.

A sauna! I wondered where a sauna was on this boat. I told Tolig that I would love to go with Tatiana to the sauna, if there would be no problem. Should we ask the commissar?

Tolig made a spitting sound. "That *kazul*? We no ask. We have plan. After work, you meet me here and I take you to Tatiana's cabin."

We finished processing the evening trawl, a small one, around 10 p.m. I met Tolig in the chi room as agreed. Reshat leaned against the doorway leading down to the crew's quarters. His casual stance belied his undercover job as look-out in this carefully choreographed plan to get me to Tatiana's cabin. Glancing nonchalantly in all directions, Reshat lifted his hand at us. Tolig pushed me forward and hurried me to the doorway.

I descended the steep stairs and stopped abruptly before the last one. Tolig crashed into me, pushing me down the final step. Now I knew how women sports reporters must feel in the locker rooms of male jocks. Male flesh filled my vision. Towels and skimpy boxer shorts thankfully covered the true jewels of these Soviet specimens of manhood.

I turned around and said fiercely, "Tolig, I cannot go here— men are in their underwear!"

He shushed me and pushed me gently forward. "No problem! No problem!"

Only a few of the men reacted with embarrassment. The rest of them greeted me with the usual shouts of "Dasha! *Dobre viecher! Peet chi!*" I quickly decided to play this scene up and pretended modesty, covering my eyes and gasping. Towels flapped and men snapped the elastic waist bands of their boxers, threatening to drop them to the floor. With a little encouragement, I am sure they would have. However, Tolig hurried me through the throngs of half-naked men toward the bow of the ship.

After leaving the men's area, we came to a single cabin. Tolig knocked on the door, and Tatiana opened it. We smiled shyly at each other. She and Tolig had a short discussion, and then she pulled me eagerly into the cabin, shutting the door behind me. The cabin was large and dim, with draped bunk beds and three separate dressers, armoires and sinks. Inhaling deeply, I savored the smell of perfume and soap. Colorful scarves were positioned around the light fixtures, filling the cabin with a subtle glow. Cheerful posters decorated the stark walls. What a difference from the drabness of the rest of the *Orekhova*. In fact, the portrait of Lenin was eclipsed by a beautiful countryside scene posted beside it.

Seated at one of the dressers was the cook I had seen in the galley. She jumped up and strode toward me, her dingy pink robe flapping around her bare legs. Smiling, she introduced herself as Marina, the assistant chef.

My eye caught the movement of an upper bunk curtain as a hand pulled it back and a dark face peaked out. Marina pointed to this woman and said, "She is Elanya—very shy." Elanya blushed and smiled at me.

Tatiana and Marina gathered around me and urged me to a chair in front of one of the dressers. Tatiana busied herself with the electric teapot in the corner of the dresser, and Marina pulled out photographs to show me.

"See, Dasha, my husband. He is cook on *MS Kronotsky*." She showed me a photograph of a handsome blonde man with a slight mustache.

"He is a cook on another boat? Why can you not cook together on the same boat?" It took a minute and language assistance from Tatiana for Marina to understand my question.

"Rules not allow wife and husband to work together." Marina smiled sadly and said something in Russian to Tatiana.

"Dasha, many people jealous if some crew have wife or husband on board. Then everyone wants this." Tatiana explained.

Marina tugged on my sleeve to show me a photograph of two smiling children, a girl and boy who looked to be about 10 or 12 years old. They were both dressed very neatly, the boy in a suit and tie and the girl in a frilly dress with a big white puffy bow in her hair.

"My children." She beamed proudly. "Son, Alexi. Daughter, Galena."

"Who takes care of them when you and your husband are at sea? When do you get to see them?" Again, Tatiana helped interpret my questions.

"Children live at my mother. She like their mother. When I come home, sometimes problems." Marina seemed saddened.

Tatiana explained that the crew worked six months of the year at sea and they had six months at home. I told her what the schedule had been like for the crew members of the *Kyowa*, and she was astonished. I asked if she liked her work and her schedule.

"Ah, Dasha. This is job. We all need jobs and job on boat is good pay. Better money for me to work on boat. Same for Marina and Elenya. I also have child." Tatiana went to her bunk and pulled a photograph from the wall. A six or seven-year old girl with a white dress and the same puffy white bow as Marina's daughter smiled at me. "My mother also take care of her."

Tatiana did not mention a husband or father, and I did not ask. I did ask if Elenya had children and was told she did not. Tatiana was 27, Marina 32 and Elenya 29. Tatiana served our tea, and we talked more about their families and their lives at sea. My balloon of idealism received a prick when I asked Tatiana about the women's work hours and salary. Were they comparable to those of the the male factory and deck workers?

Tatiana laughed. "Oh, no, Dasha. We make much less money than men. And also we must do our own jobs and to help in the factory whenever there is much fishes. So, you see, we also do more work than men." She shrugged. "Always we think this is not right. But better pay than land job, so we must accept this things."

When we had finished our tea, Tatiana went to one of the armoires and pulled out a blue robe, giving it to me to put on. She also handed me a towel. Marina and Elenya stripped off their clothes and put on robes, so I did the same. When Tatiana saw I had no slippers, she rummaged around in her armoire and found a tattered pair for me. I managed to stuff my feet into them, crossing my fingers in hopes that they would not split apart. With towels draped over our arms, Tatiana led us, like women on they way to gym class, out of the cabin. We turned left and headed closer to the bow of the ship. Though the seas were calm and the motion of the ship was minimal, being this close to the front of the boat intensified the bit of pitching that there was. My limited sea-going time had taught me that the bow of the ship experiences the most motion and the stern the least. Of course, had I known this when I first boarded the *Kyowa* and was so sick, I probably would have slept in the factory, back near the fish bins. That would not have gone over well with the officers, I'm sure.

Tatiana reached a room on our right, and she opened the door. Stepping through, I felt like I had entered the set for a horror movie. Dingy white walls surrounded me, and large white pipes snaked along the walls and ceiling. Many of them hissed steam. Streams of water trickled from others. Moldy plastic curtains slapped the walls of two partitioned stalls on my right. I wondered what scary things were hidden behind them. My attention focused on two large round metal vats with faucets that looked like cauldrons for cooking up a brew of God-knew-what. My eyes were round as I pointed to these and asked Tatiana what they were.

"Dasha, these for all ship's laundry." She pulled two wooden paddles from underneath the vats, turned on the faucet and showed me how they stirred the clothes round and round in the first vat. The second one was used for rinsing. Across the hall, she said, was the drying room where they hung everything to dry. What a relief.

"Every 10 days we must do all washing for ship. Your clothes also!" She smiled at me. After seeing how physically demanding this work was, I couldn't believe she was smiling. I also promised myself that I would make as few additions as possible to their work.

"Y'all do washing? Does anyone else help?" I found it hard to believe that the three of them were expected to do laundry for the entire ship's complement of around 45 people.

"Elenya number one washer, but it is job for Marina and me also. When we finish in kitchen, we come here to work with Elenya. Wash days big work days for us." Again, Tatiana smiled as she said this. Knowing her and Marina's primary duties were in the kitchen, I asked her if Elenya had other duties besides washing.

"Oh, yes—Elenya must to clean all bathrooms, officers' cabins, kitchens. She have big job." Elenya should have the highest salary on the ship, I thought, for having to clean those nightmarish toilets.

Marina and Elenya, having disrobed, opened a large wooden door at the front of the room. We hung our robes on hooks by the door and stepped into the sauna. It was a small space, finished in wood. More steaming, hissing pipes ran over the ceiling. The room smelled wonderfully of wet cedar, a welcome change from the fish and body odors which usually surrounded me. The sauna was actually built against the hull of the ship, right at the bow, so the slant of the wooden walls matched the curve of the ship.

Wooden benches edged into the wall, and a wooden table sat in the middle of the floor. Marina plopped face down on the table, sighing. Wielding a small tree branch with withered leaves attached to it, Tatiana stood over her like a Dominatrix.

"Birch branch is very good for health. Dasha, you next," she said as she vigorously slapped Marina all over with the lash-like twig.

I tried not to think of all of the S and M stories I had heard as I took my turn on the table, sweat pouring from my body like the water from the pipes over my head. I grinned half-heartedly up at Tatiana and pleaded with her not to be too harsh with the branch. She pushed my head down gently. Despite the heat of the sauna, as the leaves whipped my skin, a delicious cool sensation penetrated my body. It felt wonderful; relaxing and invigorating all at the same time.

Elenya lay down on the table next, and Marina pulled me along to flap back the moldy plastic shower curtains and expose shower knobs. As she cranked these, icy cold jets of rusty water escaped from the overhead nozzles. Marina twisted and turned in ecstasy. I gritted my teeth, closed my eyes and gasped as the freezing water blasted me.

We each took a few more turns, alternating between the sauna and the cold showers until I could take it no more. I think the three Soviet women could have stayed all night, but they took pity on this foreigner whose stamina for heat and cold did not match theirs. We all dried off and slipped our robes back on, then headed back to their cabin.

Tatiana pulled out bottles of Kamchatka mineral water for us and made yet another pot of tea. The four of us talked and laughed for another hour or so, thoroughly enjoying each other's company. Finally, I realized how late it was and stood to leave. Tatiana and Marina had told me they both had to be in the kitchen by 5:30 a.m., and I didn't want to interfere with their much-needed, I was sure, rest. I thanked each of them for the wonderful time and added that I hoped we could do it again.

"Oh, yes—most time men always use sauna and no women allowed. But sometimes we can get for just us. I hope again soon we can. I tell you when women can go again." Tatiana stood and we hugged each other good-bye, as did Marina and I. Elenya was too shy to hug me, so we simply said, *"Dobre noche."*

I started to leave, and Tatiana said "Wait, Dasha. Not safe—let me get Tolig."

Within a few minutes, Tolig popped his head in the cabin and motioned for me to follow him. We went back down the port-side corridor, the same way we had come in. It was quiet now, with only a few cabin doors open. Several men saw me and waved. I followed Tolig up the stairs and waited near the top while he checked out the deck. I heard him talking in a low voice to someone, and it was several minutes before he reappeared and said that we should go another way. We retraced our steps and cut through to the starboard corridor, where there were more crew members' cabins.

It was quiet on this side, as well. Whispering, I asked him why we had to go this way.

"Spuin on deck. Alexander from factory. He is no good." Tolig shook his head. I didn't know which Alexander from the factory and asked Tolig to describe him. Tolig told me he worked the flash freezers, and I was then able to place him. He was a mousy blonde man, short and thin. Now it made sense that I never saw him hanging out with the other factory men on his shift. He kept to himself—and the others did not make an effort to include him in their tea drinking, which was the socializing ritual for everyone.

The corridor to my cabin was quiet, and we tiptoed past closed doors. We reached my cabin, and I opened the door, pointing for Tolig to go in first. He came in and I whispered for him to sit down; I would make tea with my electric teapot. The commissar had managed to find me one, as well as some Kamchatka mineral water.

Before sitting down, Tolig scanned the ceiling of my room. His eyes stopped on a tiny bronze colored pipe, a half inch in diameter, with a bulb on the end of it that protruded about an inch out of the ceiling. It was situated over the couch by the porthole, and I had wondered what this was, but had not paid much attention to it. The *Orekhova* was filled with pipes, large and small, that hung from the ceiling and snaked all over the ship. Tolig put his finger to his lips and imitated wrapping something around the bulb. I pulled out a sock, and, standing on tiptoe, he tucked this around the pipe.

Finishing this task, he whispered, "Commissar listen to your room with this." My eyes widened. "No way, Tolig. I can't believe that!" Tolig shrugged his shoulders. "You see commissar has room by officer's galley? This is spuin room. He listen here and some other places."

I really could not believe this. A listening device in my cabin? For one thing, it was so terribly obvious—anyone looking would see it. Maybe, however, the best spy equipment was reserved for the Big Boys, and the fishing vessels got the left-over stuff.

Tolig told me that once, the commissar had decided to go work in the factory—to provide a good role model, I suppose. Upon hearing that he planned to do this, some of the men decided his shiny, never-used rain gear needed to be broken in. Using a needle, they poked invisible holes all over the jacket and in his rubber gloves. When he went to work, the men took great pleasure in watching him squirm as water and fish slime penetrated the tiny holes and his dry clothes became soaked.

I brewed up tea, and Tolig reached under my mattress, finding the magazines just where he had stashed them. Almost reverently, he opened the top one and slowly turned each page. I knew what he would say when he found the first advertisement, one for a Macintosh computer.

"How much this machine cost, Dasha?"

Ad after ad, picture after picture, he wanted to know the cost of each item. Every time I replied, his response was the same. His eyes widened and he shook his head. "So much money. So much money."

Tolig started yawning before I did, and I was amazed to realize it was well after midnight. We said good night and Tolig, after looking up and down the corridor, stepped quietly out and headed away, his bald head glistening under the naked light bulbs.

TWELVE

Propaganda and Peanut Butter

THE WORKLOAD ON THE *OREKHOVA* PROVED TO BE MINIMAL—A COUPLE of 5-10 ton trawls a day and that was it. I averaged about five hours in the factory and another one or two on paperwork everyday. Some days we didn't take nets at all. Work life aboard the *Orekhova* was a far cry from the endless hours and mountains of fish on the *Kyowa*.

The days settled into a pleasant pattern, despite the prying eyes and ears of the commissar and his spuins. My friends and I devised elaborate plans to evade them. Certain men were assigned lookout posts when it was time to get together in the chi room. We came up with code words for "safe," "danger," "come back again in 10 minutes."

I got constant invitations to join the captain and the other officers in his cabin for "parties," but the commissar and the factory manager always attended, so I tried to avoid these get-togethers. I enjoyed the company of Tolig and his crew much more, and Tatiana and Marina. I usually got to visit with the women only late at night, as they worked so hard during the day.

I wanted to learn Russian, and the chi room was my language center. Tolig spent hours teaching me Russian, as did Oleg, who also spoke some English. Reshat and the other men assisted when they could, mostly telling me dirty jokes and trying to get me to understand them. Humor is not easily translated; irony even less so. The Russians have many *Pagavorkas*—fables, or traditional sayings—that the men would repeat to me. Sometimes the meaning was clear, often it was not. One of my favorite *Pagavorkas* was "Work is not a wolf; it will not flee into the woods." This seemed to sum up their attitude toward work—they would get to it when they wanted to; once those fish were on board, they weren't going anywhere.

Since what I most needed to know was how to speak and understand Russian, this is the area in which I concentrated. I worked on vocabulary and rudimentary sentence structure. A spiral notebook became my dictionary, and, in English, I wrote out words and phrases phonetically. I never learned to read or write Russian, only to speak it minimally. I practiced constantly and within several weeks could carry on a basic, three-minute conversation.

I usually ended up in the chi room with Tolig and his crew after the evening trawl. We ate *kartoshkas* and drank tea. I practiced my Russian. Sometimes I brought out my tape player and we played cassettes. Oleg was an excellent guitar player and, with coaxing, he would bring his guitar up from his cabin and sing Russian folks songs for us. Occasionally, Reshat would take a turn. He sang in the Azerbijani language, which none of us could understand, but the melodies were beautiful. Reshat's singing was so expressive I felt that I knew what he was saying. With his head thrown back and his face seemingly enraptured, he transported us all to another world. But it was a world that would always remain foreign to me—a life and a history that I could never fully understand, because I came from a different world and a different place. Unless we live a life, how can we really know what it is like?

*   *   *

One evening, after Oleg had finished singing a raucous song— and fairly off-color, I gathered from the men—I brought out a treat I had been hoarding since my arrival on the *Orekhova*. Forget the Caviar and the healthy brown bread with real butter—this was a 100% American delicacy: peanut butter.

Tolig eagerly took the Jiff Crunchy Peanut Butter jar from my hands and squinted at the label. Reshat tugged at his sleeve, trying to grab the jar. The other men jumped up from their crates and clustered around Tolig, muttering in unintelligible Russian.

Tolig cleared his throat. "J-e-e-f P-e-en B-u-t-t-ah. What this, Dasha?"

Grasping a spoon in one hand, I twisted open the lid and dipped out a glob of peanut butter, offering it to Tolig. He delicately took the spoon and placed the entire contents in his open mouth. The spoon came out clean as it slid from his lips. No one said a word; all eyes were on Tolig. His mouth opened once, twice. Slowly and with difficulty. I needed oil so we could lubricate his jaws like the Tin Man in the Wizard of Oz.

By now the jar and spoon were being passed from man to man. Loud smacking sounds filled the air. Garbled words escaped through muffled lips. Reshat's eyes opened wide, and Tolig's face scrunched with the effort of still trying to swallow the sticky goo. Finally he said, "Dasha, this sweet glue taste like *orek*."

"*Orek*? Like *Orekhova*, the name of our ship?"

Tolig nodded. "*Orek* is nut—I think like your peen buttah nut."

From my pocket I pulled out the small dictionary that accompanied me everywhere. Sure enough, the word *orek* meant peanut. Oh, my God—I had been on The Peanut Ship all this time and never known it. I laughed out loud, savoring my new nickname for the *Orekhova*.

*   *   *

A couple of nights after the peanut butter tasting, the commissar was particularly insistent that I come to the crew's mess for the "*kino*," the nightly movie. Occasionally, when the crew and I wanted a change, we attended these shows. This was the one time when it was officially OK for me to be with the crew. Of course, the movies had all been picked out by the commissar. They were black and white and often anti-U.S. propaganda films. I could only understand some of the voice over, but the images were easy enough to figure out.

Once we were all settled on the benches in the crew's mess, Mikhail, the trawl master who had picked me up, barked out the order to cut the lights. The reel-to-reel projector clattered and squealed as the scene wavered onto the sheet hung in front of the mess hall. Exclamations filled the room as we all realized this movie was in color. The first 20 minutes of the film were devoted to the drudgery of life under the early Russian Czars. There were shots of peasants swinging hoes in the fields and others scrabbling in the dirt for food. More peasants, shivering in the cold winter with thin layers of ragged clothing. Next came scenes of the splendor in which the Czars and upper-class Russians lived. This was followed by the Russian Revolution and the storming of the Winter Palace in St. Petersburg. There were vivid scenes of the destruction and looting of the chandeliers, paintings, gleaming gold furniture and luxurious clothes that filled the palace. The final third of the movie showed scenes of Soviet life today—plump and smiling Soviets eating sumptuous meals in their homes. Well-dressed women shopping for food at markets whose counters overflowed with produce. Men and women hard at work in office settings.

After movie time, "my gang," as I had now come to think of Tolig and his trawl crew, would quietly adjourn to the chi room. I would go off to my cabin, wait 10-15 minutes for the coast to be clear, then join them. On this particular evening, when I finally ducked into the chi room, the men were laughing and making jokes about the movie we had just seen.

"Russian propaganda, Dasha. You like this movie?" Tolig rolled his eyes.

"I hope you not believe our lives like that movie. Look at my clothes!" Laughing, he yanked at his grubby coveralls with the rope around the waist.

Oleg interjected, "Dasha, we hear America very bad place. Everyone take drugs. Many criminals. Many people sleep on streets. Why so many problems in your country?"

I tried to explain that not everyone did those things he mentioned. Some people, yes, but not all.

"Oleg, in your country you must have people who take drugs. And crime. What problems do you have?"

"Oh, no—we have no drugs in entire Soviet Union. No crime either. No one sleeps on streets." Oleg replied earnestly.

"Oleg, all countries have these problems. Not just America. Every country in the world has people who take drugs, people who rob. Surely Soviet Union has some of these people." I said politely.

"No, not Soviet Union. We have no problems like these. I think only America have many bad things like this."

"Why do you think this, Oleg?"

"Everyday in newspaper and on TV news is stories about bad people in America. Many pictures of poor people sleeping on street. Pictures of many people putting heroin in arms. Newspaper say that every person in America have two guns."

"You believe these things, Oleg?

He looked puzzled. "Of course—it is truth. My government says it is true."

Breathing. *Thinking for myself was like breathing.* It just happened, it was a part of life. But my free thinking was not instinctual, like breathing. Somewhere I had *learned* to think for myself. My society had shaped me into a person who questioned, refusing to blindly accept what I was told, and also refusing to accept injustices. The Soviets, too, had learned. But they had learned the danger of thinking for oneself. They had learned to be afraid, to hide—and to accept, as truth, everything that their government told them. Like clay objects molded by separate artists, we were shaped into entirely different pieces.

Later, partway through one of my many cruises with the Soviets, the commissar suddenly laid down a rule that all crew members must be in their cabins by 10 p.m.—a curfew for 40 working adults. I was outraged and stunned. And I could not understand the docile acceptance of everyone around me. I questioned my closest friends on the boat, asking them if they were not angry. Surely they must want to take action against this breach of freedom, perhaps talk to the commissar as individuals or as a group. Their answers to my frustrated questioning were all the same: "There is nothing we can do. Yes, it is unfair, but *there is nothing we can do.*" Accepting this attitude was the hardest thing I had to do on my Soviet ships, because it was the most foreign to me.

Working with the Soviets over the months challenged me to define my values. I would never take freedom for granted again. Freedom, justice, liberty for all . . . before, these were just words. Words that floated about like soap bubbles from a child's plastic wand. They were shiny and beautiful but had no substance, no weight. But now they were real. Because I lived with people who did not have them. And when you experience the absence of what you value most, it becomes real to you.

THIRTEEN

Cabin Search

SIX WEEKS INTO THE CRUISE, TOLIG CAME TO ME AND SAID HE NEEDED my help. For Tolig I would do anything, and I told him so. With wide eyes, he told me a rumor was circulating among the crew that the commissar was going to do a ship-wide search and confiscate any "inappropriate," that is, American, goods that he found. There would be dire consequences for whomever was found to have any such items in their cabin. Would I hide some things in my cabin until the danger passed?

"What if the commissar searches my cabin?" I asked Tolig. "Even though he officially has no right to do so, he may. After all, we think he has it bugged."

"I think he not search observer cabin. I think he know trouble for him if he search your belongings."

I realized that even if he did search my cabin, I could claim anything he found was mine. I knew the men traded things with the catcher boats when they could get away with it. They often ended up with baseball caps, key chains and other American souvenirs, which they happily showed off to me—secretly and behind locked doors. In fact, I had given them small gifts myself— Seattle mugs, postcards, sporting magazines. I had finally persuaded Tolig to take the magazines from my cabin, once he found what he thought was a good hiding spot somewhere down below. I knew that the catcher boats sometimes secretly sent over magazines, and I was not so naive as to believe that all of them were sports magazines. I assumed their packages contained pornographic magazines and alcohol, though I had never seen any. I asked Tolig if there would be any of these in the things he wanted me to hide, telling him I would be very nervous about these items. Pornography was strictly prohibited in the USSR, and, theoretically, alcohol was prohibited on the ships. Of course, I had early on discovered what a joke the "dry boat" policy was.

Tolig looked at me silently. Then he said, "Maybe best if I give you package and you not to look at it."

God, I would be deliberately violating the policy of the Soviet government, not just some arbitrary crap the commissar had decided on. Souvenirs and coffee mugs were one thing; pornography and alcohol another. What was the right thing to do? What did I value most here? Certainly not the system that forced these people to behave like guilty criminals, hiding baseball caps and coffee mugs. And, most of all, I hated the commissar and everything he stood for. My loyalties lay with Tolig and the other crew members.

I told Tolig I would hide whatever he gave me. When was this search to happen? Did he know?

"Very soon, I think, Dasha. Tonight I give you package."

After work that evening, Tolig asked if we could meet late that night, after midnight if possible. There were fewer people about at that time.

"Should I meet you in the chi room?" I wondered at the safety of this; anyone could see me coming and going from there.

"No, no. I meet you at Tatiana's cabin. Then you can go up stairs at front."

The stairs Tolig referred to were out of the way and seldom used. The only drawback was that the egress was right beside the factory manager's cabin. But this really did seem the wisest route: foot traffic should be zero. I would just have to ensure that Fyodr's door was closed.

I asked Tolig how big the packet would be. He outlined something about three feet long and a foot wide. I hoped it would fit beneath my rain jacket, which was the bulkiest coat I had.

"Dasha, Reshat come to your cabin when safe—after midnight. Two knocks, then you know go to Tatiana."

Our conversation took place on the stern stairway that lead

out of the factory, where few people ventured. Tolig meandered back through the factory to the crew's quarters, and I headed to my cabin to clean up from processing. Instead of leaving my rain jacket in the chi room as I usually did, I kept it on after hosing it down in the factory.

I stayed in my cabin and tried to do paperwork. The busy sounds of shipboard life quieted down. The clock ticked slowly and the deep night seemed to close in on me. As midnight approached, I could feel my stomach tightening with nervousness. I paced the length of what now felt like a cell, back and forth, my body refusing to stay still. On every third round, I stopped in front of the jagged mirror and stretched my face into various grimaces. God, I couldn't believe I was doing this. Shouldn't all this time and energy, not to mention anxiety, be directed at something that really was important? Like delivering sensitive information to save a person's life or smuggling a refugee to safety? Not clandestinely meeting a contact to pick up a packet of stupid American paraphernalia. I had learned, though, that even the simplest things take on huge significance in this unreal world at sea. I stuck my head through the open porthole and breathed deeply of the cool sea air, staring up at the glittering stars to remind myself that there was another world out there.

Around 12:30 a.m., two quiet, quick knocks broke the ship's silence. I jumped towards my door and jerked it open. Peering into the corridor, I saw Reshat's back as he headed out toward the deck. He looked back, once, over his shoulder and nodded slightly.

I took my damp rain jacket from its hook and slipped it on. Quietly shutting my door, I walked quickly toward the front stairs. Both Pyotr and the factory manager's doors were shut. So far, so good. My heart raced as I tiptoed down the stairs. The crew's corridor was silent and damp. I stopped mid-step as a loud, snorting sound filled the air, muffling the soft hum of the ship's engines. Mikhail—notorious for snoring like a bear. The overhead bulbs in the corridor were out, and the darkness of the tunnel was interrupted only by patches of light from open cabin doorways. Head down, I shuffled my way to Tatiana's cabin. I knocked softly on her door. It opened a crack, and two wide brown eyes met mine. An arm snaked through the crack in the door and fingers tightly clasped my hand, pulling me forward into the cabin. Tolig sat on one of the dresser chairs. He jumped up when he saw me. He and Tatiana exchanged words, and Tatiana went to one of the armoires and extracted a large bundle wrapped in black plastic.

The bundle was fairly heavy, but I managed to tuck it under my coat and, with one arm pressed against my chest, hold it in place.

"Dasha, thank you for this. Presents for our children in there." Both Tatiana and Marina smiled gratefully at me.

Tolig checked the corridor and motioned that it was safe. I stepped out of the cabin and quickly turned left, hobbled by the packet. I sidestepped up the stairs, the bundle threatening to slide from beneath my coat, and looked out into the corridor. Clear. The factory master's door was still closed, as was Pyotr's. I eased quietly into my cabin, just as the bundle slipped from my tenuous grasp to the floor.

Now, where to stash the thing. Armoire? No, too obvious. And it wouldn't fit in the drawer under the bunk bed. Perhaps tucked under my mattress? No, too bulky—I would never sleep. I finally decided to wrap it in clothes and other items and put it in my duffel bag, which was laid across the top bunk. It was a perfect fit for the bag, and my duffel was the one place that the commissar would have no right to check. It was solely my personal property, unlike the armoire or bunk drawer.

I camouflaged the package as best I could, tucked it into the duffel and zipped the bag shut. My adrenaline was still pumping, but I forced myself to crawl into my bottom bunk and lie down. When I finally slept, I dreamed that I was being pursued across a vast wasteland that changed from rocky desert to mountainous snow field. Frightened and frozen, I had no idea what my pursuer looked like, only the terrifying feeling that I could never really escape.

* * *

The tension on the boat was palpable the next day. My world felt heavy and oppressive. I knew there was something else out there, back in the United States, where paranoia and fear didn't surround me. But I could not grasp it; it seemed hazy and very far away. I could not remember what it felt like not to be fearful and anxious.

I had taken to being on deck as the nets were brought on board. Since the tonnages were so small, it was easier to get a close look at what the trawl contained by watching as the men dumped it into the bins. I stood on deck, shifting from foot to foot and waiting to pick up our first net, my stomach in knots. I had visions of the commissar slipping into my cabin, rifling my belongings, and discovering the hidden bundle. He knew my work habits—I would be away from my cabin for 3-4 hours now. Plenty of time for him to do a leisurely search.

The trawl crew arrived on deck to pick up the net. Tolig told me that the search had not yet taken place, but the commissar was going to have an all-ship meeting in the crew's mess in the afternoon. The commissar regularly held Communist Party meetings, which most of the crew members attended. Only a handful of the ship's crew were not party members, Tolig and Reshat among them.

After my factory work, I raced back to my cabin to check on the bundle. It was in its place, seemingly undisturbed.

At 1 p.m., the doors to the crew's mess slammed shut and the empty corridors of the *Orekhova* echoed silently as I nervously roamed them. I passed the forbidding doors and heard the commissar's voice, muffled but definitely raised in anger. I headed up to the bridge, where Pyotr stood watch; someone had to be there, even though we were dead in the water. I asked him if he were sorry to be missing the meeting. He spat out of the side of his mouth and rattled off a string of Russian words, a few of which I recognized as curse words.

I went back to my cabin to try to concentrate on paperwork, a hopeless task. Mostly, I hung my head out of the porthole, telling myself that the real world—my real world, at any rate—lay out there somewhere. Eventually, I heard voices and people walking by my closed door. If the commissar and his cronies were going to search, I figured I was in a good spot. Surely, he wouldn't dare come into my cabin while I was there.

A couple of hours later, there was a knock on my door. Taking a deep breath, I yanked the door open. Tolig's tense face greeted me, and he jerked his head for me to follow him. Quickly we made our way to the chi room.

Reshat and the rest of the deck crew sat on their usual crates, talking quietly but heatedly. Tolig patted the crate beside him, and I sat down. Reshat told Tolig to double check the door.

Tolig started in, "So, commissar have big meeting. He ask who have American things. Everyone silent. He ask three more times—silence every time. Then he ask special people." I had an idea of what "special people" meant.

"Me, Reshat, Tatiana, some others. We all say nothing. Then commissar say he will search all cabins. Alexander, Fyodr, Mikhail and commissar all come to crew cabins and look at everything. But they find nothing. Commissar very angry." Here the men started laughing and imitating the commissar in his angry state. "Then—finish."

"What do you think will happen now?" I asked Tolig.

"I think maybe finish. No more looking. Now OK."

Tolig asked me to keep the packet until they felt it was safe; he would let me know when I could return it.

Two days later, I returned the packet to Tatiana's cabin, doing it in much the same way I had picked it up. The commissar never said a word to me about the search; he did ask me to refrain from sharing my magazines with the crew and not to give them any gifts of American items. I simply agreed to abide by his request, not disclosing that I had already given souvenirs to my friends.

Life on the *Orekhova* slowly returned to normal. Instead of political harassment, we went back to fishing, picking up our two nets each day. I continued to spend evenings in the chi room, laughing and talking with my friends, but always aware that our easy camaraderie could be disrupted at any moment.

* * *

After ten weeks on the Orekhova, I received a radio message from NMFS, requesting that I return to shore. They would be sending a replacement observer, and I needed to arrange the transfer with one of the catcher boats with whom we worked.

I felt a confusion of emotions upon receiving the message: relief that I could return to a normal way of life, free of paranoia and fear and oppression; a wrenching sadness at the thought of leaving my friend, Tolig, and the other crew members. I couldn't think what it would be like not to see Tolig and Reshat, Tatiana and Marina everyday. They had become such a part of me. Strangely, I felt guilty. For me, this was a temporary experiment at Soviet living, a piece of adventure that I would fold into my life with all of my other experiences. The Soviets did not have this luxury. They would never slip through the bars of the cage that allowed them only to glimpse an outside world but never to become part of it.

Word traveled quickly on the boat that I would soon be leaving. Tolig came to me, his brown eyes full of sadness, and asked if it were true. Tatiana and Marina brought gifts of lace handkerchiefs that they had embroidered. Pyotr gave me a heavy metal cassette tape, for which I laughingly thanked him. All the while, I fought to keep back the tears that threatened to cascade down my cheeks.

Via radio, I arranged to go back into Dutch Harbor on the *American Dream*, a catcher boat that was returning in two days to change crew members. We were to meet them at a designated spot around 10:00 on the morning of August 5; it would take us a couple of days to get back to Dutch. Tolig made me promise that my last night would be spent with the gang; they wanted to have a party in the crew's quarters, probably in the cabin he and Reshat shared. I could think of nowhere else I would rather be on my last night on the *Orekhova*.

The commissar, however, had other plans. Precisely because he knew where I wanted to be, I was sure, he told me that he and the captain would be having a farewell party for me on my last night. In the captain's cabin, where my welcome aboard party had been. There was no way I could gracefully get out of this; I would have to attend.

My last night came all too quickly. The commissar summoned me to the captain's cabin around 7:30 p.m. Taking the empty seat beside the captain, I looked around the lavishly spread table at the faces that had become so familiar to me. The forever winking chief mate, who grinned and, of course, blinked that right eye at me. Galena, the doctor, who always seemed anxious to befriend me. The men had told me, however, that she was close to the commissar, so I had kept my distance. The captain, who had turned out to be a kind and useless fellow. I had rarely seen him, and when I did, he was either drunk or hung over. Tolig told me that the captain hated the commissar and was really a good man, just drinking to escape dealing with all of the political crap. The radio officer, a nice man who had shown me his family photographs and spoken lovingly of his wife and two children at home. Fyodr, the vulture of a factory manager. Or, at least, theoretically the factory manager. In reality he and the commissar were as tight as peas in a pod, just as Tolig had originally told me they were.

The party proceeded just as the one two months ago had. First we acceptably drank Kamchatka mineral water. An hour or so into it, Tatiana, who had been serving us, was dismissed. The door was locked, music turned up and out came the bottles of vodka. Everyone at the table, except me, downed glass after glass of vodka. Fairly soon the effects began to show. I knew it would take awhile for me to extricate myself, so I began attempting to do so within the next hour.

"No, no, Dasha—your last night! More toasts!" The captain raised his glass. After three more aborted attempts, I was finally able to get away. I had been watching the commissar carefully, and he had imbibed a good quantity of vodka. I hoped this would put him out for the rest of the night.

As we had agreed earlier, I went straight downstairs to Tolig and Reshat's cabin. They were expecting me as soon as I could get away. When I arrived, they flung the door open and welcomed me excitedly. All of my friends were there—Tolig's crew, Tatiana and Marina, Pyotr. I first had to give them a report on the captain's party. They wanted to hear, in detail, about the sumptuous food and alcohol. Since they were not allowed either of these, I wondered why they wanted to torture themselves. But tonight they fooled me and pulled out, from various hidden spots, cans of Miller Beer. These same cans had probably been hidden in my duffel bag on that fateful day of the search. Reshat opened his armoire and motioned me over to look at a large glass jar full of a thick, evil looking brown liquid. He stirred it a few times and set it on the table.

"*Somogon*." He replied when I asked him what this was. There was laughter all around, and Tatiana told me that *Somogon* was "secret Russian alcohol." Ahh—moonshine. As best I could understand, *Somogon* was made from fermented bread. Reshat had been working on this jar for some time. I was offered the first glass, which I dutifully tasted. I immediately grimaced, which sent the room into fits of laughter. This stuff tasted like moldy bread and smelled like dirty socks.

"Please, Kamchatka mineral water!" I laughed. Tolig said Kamchatka mineral water would, from then on aboard the *Orekhova*, be called "Dasha's Beer." The party got into full swing, with all of us crammed into that tiny cabin. We were close this night, in more ways than one. Oleg pulled out a guitar and began to sing— those melancholy Russian ballads that, this night, brought tears to my eyes. I looked around at the faces of these people. My friends—funny, kind, loving and generous. How could they be these things when their world did everything it could to drive the very life out of them?

*   *   *

By 10:00 the next morning, I was packed and standing by the deck railing. My eyes burned from lack of sleep and too much crying. My friends surrounded me. To ease the somber mood, we joked with each other. Tolig, having found out many of my secrets, teased me about how much ice cream I would eat when I got back to Seattle. He counted aloud the number of chocolate chip cookies he thought I would consume—shouting out the number of kilos I would probably add to my weight if I did so.

I pulled out my last remaining jar of peanut butter, and we stood around spooning it out and eating it, laughing as we remembered the Russians' first taste of this strange treat, and my christening of the *Orekhova* as "The Peanut Ship." I was going to miss like hell this peanut ship.

Reshat tugged at my sleeve, pointing to a small boat, the *American Dream*, moving quickly towards us. Time was running out. I took last minute photographs of my friends. Marina came running from the galley with four loaves of the freshly baked brown bread that I loved so much. More bottles of the famous Kamchatka mineral water clanked their way into my small knapsack of fragile items. Tolig presented me with my favorite pin yet—*"Malinky* Lenin"—little Lenin. The pin itself was a small red star. Embedded in its center was a tiny black-and-white photograph of a young Lenin. Oleg excitedly explained that this badge was given to young Komsomuls—young Communist Party members—who were hard workers.

Mikhail whistled Tolig over to assist him in releasing the *Orekhova's* lifeboat. Mikhail would be driving me to the catcher boat, just as he had picked me up. The *American Dream* set anchor, a stone's throw away. It was time for me to go. A wave of sadness passed over me. God, we had been through so much together.

I hugged Reshat, Pyotr, Oleg. Tatiana and Marina were crying, which made me cry as well. I had hoped to be able to hold back the tears, but I could not. The captain gave me a big bear hug, as did the chief mate. Both the commissar and Fyodr broke through the circle of my friends and stepped forward. Steeling myself, I stuck out my hand, first shaking the commissar's hand, then Fyodr's. I forced myself to politely thank them for their assistance and resisted the urge to wipe my hand off on my coveralls.

Tolig stood by the lifeboat. Mikhail had already climbed through the porthole entrance. I threw my arms around Tolig, wishing I never had to let him go. The catcher boat sounded its horn. I released Tolig to see tears sliding from his brown eyes. I rubbed the top of his soft, shiny head, smiling at him through my own tears. We looked at each other for a long moment, then he helped me climb through the porthole.

Before I disappeared into the depths of the lifeboat/submarine, Tolig said quietly "I never forget you, Dasha."

"I never forget you, Tolig. Always I will keep you here." I tapped my heart and smiled.

He clanked the porthole shut, and we swung down the side of the *Orekhova* and splashed into the ocean.

Mikhail chugged us over to the *American Dream* and we bumped against its side. Someone threw open the porthole, and I stood on tiptoe, poking my tearstained face out. Mikhail pushed my gear up through his porthole. I wiggled through mine and hoisted myself onto the deck of the catcher boat. My upper body strength had certainly improved from slinging all of those heavy baskets of fish around. I smiled as I watched Mikhail and one of the catcher boat's crew members discretely exchange small packages.

I said good-bye to Mikhail and he waved vigorously, grinning. I watched as he motored back to the *Orekhova*. The *American Dream* pulled up anchor, started its engines and began to chug away. Leaning against the railing, I waved fiercely, and the crew members lining the deck of the *Orekhova* did the same. Tolig stood alone. He was smiling slightly, clutching his battered cap in his hand. Our gazes held. I heard Reshat, Tatiana and others shouting good-bye, but I never stopped looking at Tolig. And I didn't stop waving until I finally lost sight of The Peanut Ship.

FOURTEEN

Galley Fight

I WORKED OFF AND ON AS AN OBSERVER FOR NMFS, AND TWO YEARS later joined the New Zealand observer program to work for the Ministry of Agriculture and Fisheries (MAF). I lived and worked in New Zealand for a year and a half. I spent two to four months at sea, then came ashore and traveled for a month or two, exploring every inch of the country's two main islands. I came to love New Zealand and its rugged beauty.

Seasons in New Zealand are the reverse of ours. In the winter month of June I was assigned to the *Akagi Maru.* The New Zealand observer program placed two observers on a boat, and my coworker was a woman named Rosalind Squires. We got on well, and both of us felt we'd landed on our feet aboard the *Akagi.*

The *Akagi* was 90 meters long, about 270 feet—almost twice the size of the *Kyowa Maru.* It was owned by one of the most prosperous fishing companies in Japan, and this showed in every inch of the vessel. Roz and I each had our own spacious cabins which were cleaned every three days by a cabin boy, Suetosan, who also assisted in the kitchen. Suetosan washed our sheets twice a week. I often thought back to the *Orekhova* and how, at the end of 10 days, the scent rising from my bedding resembled a cross between a heap of sweaty exercise clothes and a fish market that had never passed inspection by the health department.

Saturday nights on the *Akagi* we ate lobster or steak—a whole one each. The rest of the week we had to be content with dishes of fish, flank steak, chicken and vegetables. Tanaguchisan, the chief cook, and Iidasan, his assistant, carefully prepared each dish.

Suetosan would place them before us, where they gleamed like photographs from a Japanese culinary magazine. The centerpiece would perhaps be a piece of tuna sushi, perfectly sliced into thin, even sections and placed so that the pinkish red flesh glistened in the galley lights. Pencil thin strips of daikon, a mild radish, lay like sunbeams radiating outward from the fish. Other unfamiliar vegetables were carefully arranged to add color and texture to the exquisite design. The globs of fried fish and small scraps of canned vegetables on the *Kyowa* seemed far away.

I sometimes wondered how different a luxury cruise would be from my life on the *Akagi*. Early on, Sasakisan, the chief officer, had seen me in my cabin listening to my walkman. Minutes later, he tapped on my door and entered with a large cassette tape player with removable speakers. Picking up the telephone, he summoned the second officer, Satomurasan, to my cabin and they poked and wriggled around until they had installed the player on my desk and the speakers in stereo position. Now classical music soothed me from all directions.

On day one, Suetosan presented Roz and me with large, fluffy towels and a sign that read, in English, "Take bath observer." A huge hot tub stood in the middle of the bathing area floor and a shower provided endless supplies of fresh, hot water. When I emerged from bathing, I felt like I had just ended a spa session. I loved my soft, clean skin, so different from the salt-encrusted feeling I always had on the *Kyowa*, with its lack of fresh water. My hair stopped looking like the winter coat of a hibernating bear; it dried to a shiny glow and no longer felt like a matted wool cap on my head.

Roz was a night owl and volunteered to work the night shift. I had the unbelievable luxury of sleeping through the night. I still woke with every change of sound and motion of the boat, though. Deep into the night, I would startle awake and lie very still, my entire body alert to the movement of the ship, listening for the slight difference in sound, trying to determine what we were doing. It always took a few minutes for my brain to catch up to my instincts and for me to relax back into sleep, knowing that I was not responsible, this time, for whatever activity the ship was engaging in.

The pattern of social adjustment, I had discovered, was the same on all of my ships. My first few weeks on board, I would scatter myself about, sampling all of the different folks with whom I might spend my free time, rather like going into a bakery and trying small bites of the goodies on display. Each one offered something different—some tastes I loved, some surprised me and others I choked on. Shortbreads I would fight for; anything flavored with aniseed I turned away from. The boat was like the bakery—after enough testing, I would discover my shortbreads and my aniseed items.

On the *Akagi*, the cooks were the special baked goods that both Roz and I loved. We spent evenings when we were not working hanging out in the galley with Tanaguchi, Iida and Sueto. Had I not known that Tanaguchi and Iida were cooks, I would have thought they were sumo wrestlers. Both men were about 5 1/2 feet tall and easily weighed at least 300 pounds, with Iida probably tipping the scales at a bit more. Tanaguchi's seniority was symbolized by his white sailor-like cap, which he never removed, even when he was off duty. Like the star on top of a Christmas tree, his white hat seemed permanently perched on his bald head. Iida had one of the gentlest dispositions I have ever come across. He had a special talent for remaining calm in the face of crisis. Sueto was a hummingbird, he flitted from spot to spot, buzzing incessantly, never still for long. He was reed thin and would probably have fit, folded up, in one of my sampling baskets.

Often the radio officer joined us in our evening gatherings. A stern looking man with bristling gray hair and wire rimmed glasses, his appearance belied his manner. When he arrived, our little group became even more raucous than usual.

If you have intimate knowledge of a bakery—working there, say, rather than just being a customer—you learn how to combine ingredients to come up with just the right mix for a delicious product. You also learn what ingredients are disastrous in combination. So it was with my boats. And so it was with the captain and our little group, falling into the "disastrous combination" category.

The captain of the *Akagi* could have stepped out of a fashion advertisement for *GQ* magazine. He always wore perfectly starched shirts of blinding white or soothing pastels. His khaki pants shone spotlessly, and creases fell in just the right places. Alligator belts strained to tame his girth. This distracting paunch, however, and his unfortunate hairstyle were the two reasons the *GQ* photographers would never seek him out. The captain was balding on top and oily wisps of hair lay across his shiny crown. His remaining hair, which seemed abundant, looked cut with dull hedge clippers. Tufts stuck out at different spots, some seemingly greased into sharp points and others looking like dandelion fluff, only of a dark color.

The captain's English was minimal but functional. He had the unusual habit of, when in conversation with either Roz or me, spelling out random words shortly after he had pronounced them.

"In the log book, we record fish we catch. Log book: L-o-g-b-o-o-k."

"Net stuck on bottom today because of rock. Because: B-e-c-a-u-s-e."

My interactions with the captain were always stiff and formal, like his shirts. We discussed nothing but business. Sometimes I corrected his spelling.

"Miss Dairusan, radio message sent this morning. Message: m-a-s-s-a-g-e."

"Thank you for sending my message, captain. Message: m-*e*-s-s-a-g-e."

Roz, on the other hand, could never seem to have a business conversation with the captain. After a week, it became clear he had a severe crush on her. Whenever she was on the bridge, he would appear, coming to stand close to her and recite his mantra:

"Miss Rozsan, you very beautiful. Beautiful: B-e-a-u-t-i-f-u-l."

Other times, Roz would look up from paperwork in her cabin and the captain would be hovering in her doorway, grinning like a 15-year old. Shyly, he would hold out an offering—usually sweets or an inexpensive piece of jewelry.

I discovered the captain's drinking problem by accident one night. Roz had just relieved me in the factory, and it was well after the usual dinner hour. I figured I would change clothes and then go dine with the cooks, who sat down to eat after everyone else was finished and the galley was empty. As I splashed water on my face, a frantic knocking sounded on my cabin door. I opened it to find Sueto, still in his kitchen assistant's uniform, anxiously hopping from foot to foot. His eyes were round and sweat stood out on his brow.

"Miss Dairusan, eating late because now captain many, many drink." He lifted his apron and wiped his forehead. "Not good when captain many, many drink. Big problems."

Not wanting to add to his stress, I told him that I was fine to eat dinner whenever and not to worry about me. Sueto bowed and scurried away toward the galley.

Forty-five minutes passed, and I was having trouble ignoring my rumbling stomach. I decided to wander to the galley. Stealthily I approached the dining area, not knowing what I might find. I peaked into the open doorway and saw the captain, sitting alone. He was facing me, and his eyes were closed. He swayed slightly, back and forth, as if caught in a gentle breeze. His head dipped down toward the tabletop then jerked back up abruptly. His eyes never opened. A sharp pang of feeling flooded my body. Usually I found the captain a comical character, spelling aloud arbitrary words and following Roz around like a confused adolescent. Tonight I saw him as pitiful—alone and drinking himself into a stupor. Slowly, he leaned to the right, and, like a tree toppling over in slow motion, he fell sideways onto the padded bench. I heard a noise that was muffled by the plastic tablecloth but still distinct enough for me to recognize as a sob.

*   *   *

For five days, no one saw the captain. Tanaguchi and Iida told me he had remained passed out on the galley seat for several hours and, finally, they had hefted him onto their shoulders and carried him, prostrate, to his cabin. No one seemed to know when he might again make an appearance.

This evening, the members of our little group were in our usual chummy positions in the galley. I was warm and cozy between the two slabs of Tanaguchi and Iida. Roz, the radio master and Sueto sat across the table from us. On the television screen, Scarlett O'Hara swished her skirts and said, in Japanese, "But Rhett, whatever will I do?" A movement to my left caught my eye, and I turned to catch the full force of the captain's blazing eyes. But he wasn't interested in me or even Roz. He stepped into the galley, brandishing a liquor bottle in one hand, and screamed something unintelligible at the radio officer. Scarlett and Rhett faded into the background as the radio master rose from his seat, shouting back at the captain. The captain raised the bottle threateningly, his face a mottled red. Sueto, just left of the captain, jumped on his chair, bringing himself face to face with the captain and yelling more unintelligible words right into his face. I was not sure what I was witnessing, but it was clearly bigger than this room and the current group gathered here.

The captain heaved the liquor bottle straight at the radio officer, who ducked. Roz screamed as glass shattered against the wall. The smell of alcohol wafted through the air. Tanaguchi picked up his glass and lobbed it toward the captain.

"Roz, get under the table!" I hissed as I dropped to the ground. Roz ducked out of the battle zone and joined me.

"Why are they doing this? What the hell is this all about? They're going to bloody kill each other!" She shrieked in my ear. We heard more glass shattering, followed by the thud of a body landing on the table top. More cursing and screaming. I felt suspended between two worlds. Common sense told me to get out of this fray, it was not mine. But I could not let these men kill each other. I only understood an occasional word in the free-for-all of curses that danced above me; I grasped, "work, serious, job."

Then I heard Iidasan's voice, calm and soothing. He repeated something over and over; succeeding in quieting the harsh voices of everyone around him. Iidasan's soft murmur continued to buzz and hum above us. Footsteps moved out of the galley. One set, then another and another. Iidasan peered under the table, motioning us out.

"Please, come up now. Everything all right now."

I crawled out of the left end of the table and Roz emerged from the other side. Iidasan shook his head worriedly.

"This what happens when captain drink too much. Very bad."

Iidasan told us that the captain had long hated the radio officer. This was not the first time the two had gotten into a fight. The captain was also jealous because we spent so much time with the cooks and the radio officer. Most of all, it seemed, he was upset that Roz paid him only minimal attention, and he decided to take his frustration out on the folks who claimed her full attention.

I wondered how things would be tomorrow. Would Tanaguchi and Sueto regret their severe breech of cultural rules? I still could not believe that each of them had, basically, assaulted the captain. Would the captain be embarrassed at his behavior? Would we even see him? Roz and I tiptoed off to our cabins, moving quietly and carefully so as to avoid anyone who had been part of the fray.

FIFTEEN

Fear

I QUICKLY FORGOT ABOUT THE GALLEY FIGHT. THE NEXT MORNING I was startled awake as the ship rolled sharply. I sat up and fell against the port wall as we tilted crazily to the left. The ocean poured through my closed porthole and drenched me. As the ship dipped deeply down to the right, I grabbed for the sill of the window but missed. I was thrown out of bed and skidded across the floor, wet with salt water. I watched helplessly as notebooks, coffee mugs, cassette tapes, pens and pencils took flight, then crashed into corners around me. In other parts of the ship, heavy items fell, sounding like thunder. Glass shattered; dishes in the galley, I guessed.

Pulling myself up, I shakily hugged the wall for support. The door to my closet flapped open, exposing clothes no longer draped over hangers but heaped on the floor. I scrabbled for my coveralls, balancing on one leg as I pulled them on.

I rolled down the corridor, holding the handrails that lined the walls, trying to match my foot shuffles to the movements of the ship.

On the bridge, the chief officer crouched over the chart table. The third mate pressed his nose against the front window, attempting to see through the sheets of rain slamming into the glass. Laughter cackled from the VHF radio, and I realized the fishing master was speaking with someone on another boat.

"Ah, Miss Dairusan. Bad storm now. No fishing this morning. But maybe this afternoon, weather will be OK for fishing again." The chief officer smiled at me.

"What was that big roll just now? Is everything OK?" I leaned sharply to my left, arms out flung, to demonstrate the question.

The chief officer laughed, unconcerned. "Just part of storm, Miss Dairusan. Not to worry. *Akagi Maru* is very big ship, so no problem."

I had learned that nothing phased the Japanese at sea. In bad storms, when I paced trying to calm my nervousness as we tossed and rolled, the men around me carried on as usual, laughing at my worry. I told myself that I should trust their years of sea-going experience, especially compared to my greenhorn status. If they insisted that there was nothing to worry about, I would try to follow suit. Sometimes, however, I wondered if their bravado masked a real terror. Or perhaps they really were fearless. Their nonchalance seemed genuine, and I came to rely on this attitude to keep my own in perspective.

By noon, the *Akagi Maru* had become a small mouse at the mercy of a large lion. First we were swatted from side to side, then we bounced forward as the predator toyed with us. On a whim, we rose up, up into the sky, slamming down onto an ocean that had turned into concrete. Every time we smashed into the unyielding surface, my entire body reverberated from the jarring impact. My head ached, but I didn't know if it was from the low pressure system or the pounding. I kept waiting for the onslaught of nausea, but it never came. Instead, I felt dizzy and fuzzy.

From the bridge, I watched the nose of the *Akagi* bury itself in the frothing ocean as we lunged forward. Only the glass window separated me from the sea as it engulfed the bridge. I felt trapped in a cage, the ocean threatening any minute to break the matchstick bars and devour me.

I moved toward the aft bridge window and looked down just as a huge wave thrust its way up the deck, burying winches and stacks of nets. Blinking, I shook my head in disbelief—two black-suited men flailed in the surge below me. The retreating wave sucked the figures toward the stern ramp. Suddenly they jerked to a stop, and I saw the taut lifeline running from their waists to the deck railing. Like grasshoppers, they jumped onto a pile of netting and began securing it to the railing with heavy rope, racing to beat the next crush of water.

I was jolted back to reality by the laugh of the chief officer beside me. "Ha—look at those two, they are like rats in the rain!"

He seemed to find the whole scene comical, whereas I felt sorry for the men and worried for their safety. I mentioned this to the chief officer, and he laughed merrily.

"Ah, Miss Dairusan, you worry too much. Those men have been on deck many times in bad storms. No problem! They finish making nets tight and then back inside. No problem!"

I wanted to try and make real the mountains of monstrous waves that kept attacking us. I asked the chief officer what he estimated their heights to be.

"I think maybe 15 to 20 meters tall. These very big waves." He shrugged his shoulders, unimpressed.

As I struggled back to my cabin, I mentally did the math. One meter equals about three feet, so those waves were around 50 feet tall. About the height of a five story building. I was impressed, even if the chief officer was not.

The weak, gray daylight surrendered as darkness closed in. Still the storm raged. Roz and I pulled ourselves down the corridor to the dining room, where the cooks struggled valiantly to prepare the evening meal. The non-skid surface of the dining table was designed specifically for seas like this. In case the non-skid element failed, the entire table was ringed by a half-inch high wooden "railing." Seuto danced in from the kitchen and set down our teacups, which immediately turned over and rolled into the railing. He returned to the kitchen and came back with two plates of steaming food. Just as he leaned over to set them in front of us, we rolled severely to port. Seuto fell onto Roz, folding her onto the table, the plates of food upending onto its surface. Sticky rice and pieces of fish bounced in front of me.

Sueto jumped back, apologizing profusely, his face burning with embarrassment. Laughing, Roz and I scraped up the food and dumped it back on the dishes. Sueto insisted on bringing us new plates of food, which I ate not because I was hungry but simply for lack of anything else to do.

By pulling the blankets from my bunk, I had made a nest on the floor of my cabin. I sat with my back against the bottom of the bunk and my feet against the legs of my desk, which were screwed into the floor. This way I could brace myself against the rolling of the ship. I was in this position, listening to music, when there was a knock on my door and it opened to reveal the chief officer. The relaxed, laughing demeanor from the bridge was gone. His expression was tight and his eyes appeared round and very large in his face. He closed and opened them slowly.

"Ah, Miss Dairusan, you know where your life boat station is?"

A huge crack tore through my protective shield, the one that kept all of my fears and outlawed thoughts tightly contained. I had never, ever seen a Japanese fisherman express concern about a storm. And now the chief officer was worried.

I heaved myself up from the floor and stood beside the chief officer as he pointed out the lifeboat locations, using the chart posted on the back of my door. He tapped number 3 and told me that this was my lifeboat. If I heard the alarm ring, I should go immediately to this boat.

"Ah, Miss Dairusan, you understand? You go very fast to this boat if bell rings." His black eyes drilled into me.

I nodded. Outrageous images of clinging to the orange life raft, of being tossed into the air like rice at a wedding, filled my head. I felt my inner barrier shift again; the terrifying thought of being trapped in my cabin as the *Akagi* capsized spilled into my consciousness. I thought I might throw up, and I knew it was not from seasickness.

The chief officer left and I opened my closet door, dragging out the canvas bag that contained my survival suit. I pulled out the suit and unrolled it, spreading it out on the floor beside my nest.

My fear was like a roller coaster, twisting and diving, knotting my stomach and making me wish only one thing: that this horrifying ride would please, please be over with. I remembered my last roller coaster ride. I was about 13 and friends and I were at the state fair in Raleigh. After a supper of hot dogs and cotton candy, we made our way to the looming, tangled metal structure that was billed as the most terrifying ride in the South. I gazed up at the mountains of twisted steel, screams from a torture-chamber raining down on me. My friend and I squeezed into a tiny seat, the attendant strapping us in with thin webbed seat belts. I recalled the screech of metal against metal as we rolled forward, the night air filled with nervous laughter. And then it began. The slow, steep ascent, allowing endless time to anticipate the horror of what would follow. The worst part was that it seemed to have no end: the sudden leaps, the gut-wrenching plunges straight down. I thought I was doomed to stay on this endless loop of terror, my only relief coming when I finally died from my fear.

I felt the same way now. This storm had already tortured us for 15 hours. Would we ever escape it? Was this ship my fate, my endless loop of terror? I huddled in my nest, my body braced against the unpredictable rolling of this capricious monster.

Sometime in the night I jerked awake, my body cramped against the legs of my desk. I could not feel my left arm and reached around with my right to pull it from beneath my body. I lay still, focusing on the movement and sounds of the ship. What was different? My legs were relaxed, not wedged against the desk. My body was not rolling from side to side. The sound—what was that sound? I realized it was not *a* sound but the lack of sound—the wind was no longer shrieking and howling. The soft growl of the engines had taken its place.

I smiled as I crawled up into my bunk, pulling my nest of covers from the floor. I remembered when I got off of that deadly roller coaster many years ago: my body swaying, unused to stillness, my legs wobbling and weak, and, best of all, the feel of the hard, lumpy earth under my feet. I could almost pretend that I was safe, on that solid ground once again.

SIXTEEN

The Captain's Dinner Party

IN NEW ZEALAND, UNLIKE ALASKA, FOREIGN SHIPS FISH RELATIVELY close to shore, especially during hoki season, which begins at the end of June. Hoki are a silver, elongated fish with sharp, barracuda-like teeth. They run off the west coast of New Zealand's South Island and, along with orange roughy, are the major fishery of the country. For the Japanese market, they are as popular as Bering Sea pollock.

When the hoki are running, hundreds of vessels crowd the fishing grounds, and everyone fishes round the clock. Ships process trawl after trawl, and when the fish holds are full, trawlers radio for a transport vessel so they can offload their catch. Transport vessels cruise up and down the coast, tying up to fully loaded ships and taking on their 25-kilo boxes of frozen hoki. When the transport ship is full, it offloads the catch at the shore-based processing plant.

The New Zealand Ministry of Agriculture and Fisheries sent special officers out on the transport vessels to monitor these transshipments. Basically, they counted boxes and made sure their count matched what the ship reported it was offloading. These officers always conferred with the observers on the fishing vessel, comparing our figures to what they came up with. At the end of transshipment, the officers generally came onto the fishing trawler to sample the ship's hospitality.

This time, the *Akagi* had just finished offloading its catch. Suetosan found Roz and me relaxing in our cabins. Transshipment was always a holiday for us, as there were no nets being brought on board.

"Rozsan, Dairusan—please, the captain wishes you to come to his cabin for small party with Mr. Tom and Mr. Michael."

Tom and Michael were the two transshipment monitors. Earlier I had watched the men of the *Akagi* gasp and nudge each other when Michael appeared on the deck of the transport boat. He stood nearly seven feet tall and a bush of carroty red hair sprouted from his head. I wondered how he slept in the under six-foot bunks of the Japanese ship. By contrast, Tom was slightly shorter than I was and had curly blonde hair. The extra weight he carried seemed to cause him to move slowly and clumsily on the deck of the transport ship.

Roz and I dutifully followed Seuto up to the captain's cabin. He opened the door, and ushered us into the small but luxurious space. The captain's cabin was really two spaces—one where he slept and the other where he engaged in whatever else it was that he did. Roz and I had never been able to figure out what this might be, except drinking a lot and disappearing for days at a time. The fishing operations of the *Akagi* were handled by the chief officer and fishing master. In fact, when the captain did put in a rare appearance on the bridge, it seemed to wreak havoc. A week before, we had tied up to another Japanese boat for a brief exchange of goods. When it came time to untie the *Akagi* and move away from the other ship, the captain, on the bridge in his drunken state, had insisted that the ship be turned to starboard, though both the chief officer and second mate had argued that a port turn was called for. The captain, grabbing the steering wheel, had shoved the chief officer aside, shouting "I am the captain, you will do as I say!!" He yanked the wheel and the *Akagi's* port side rammed into the bow of the other ship. For two days after this crash, *Akagi* crewmen had worked to repair the damage done to equipment on the deck.

Roz and I stood uncertainly by the door, until Sueto prodded us forward.

Standing on tiptoe, he whispered in my ear "Captain is in

bathroom. He wants you please to sit down. He will come in short time."

Now we had to play the seating game. Whenever we got trapped in these events with the captain, Roz waited to see which seat the captain took so she could position herself far away. She found it easier to take his mooning eyes and longing sighs if she were not sitting right next to him.

"Bloody hell, where is he? I don't want to sit down until he comes out." Roz hissed and rolled her eyes.

"This must be it . . . that bloke pointed up these stairs when I said 'Captain.'" A kiwi accent boomed in the corridor. A bright red head poked through the doorway. "G'day Dail! G'day Roz! I see we've found the captain's cabin." Michael grinned at us and twisted, pretzel-like, into the cabin. He stood stooped over, dwarfing everything around him. Tom lumbered in after him and greeted us.

I felt intruded upon by these foreign-seeming men. My world on the *Akagi* was comfortable and predictable. After two months, I was very possessive of its isolation and not eager to have my comfortable routine interrupted by these awkward strangers. They seemed to take up most of the space and Michael's voice crashed about the room like cymbals clashing together.

"Oh, perfect—let's arrange the seating now!" Roz gleefully directed Tom to the far side of the table. She took the chair next to him. Mike and I took the chairs nearest the door. Two chairs remained, both at the far end of the table from Roz.

The curtain separating the living room from the sleeping area swished aside, and the captain swayed across the threshold, grinning broadly. His sparse hair, which normally lay plastered across the top of his skull, now jutted across it in uneven spikes, like lines of haphazard fencing. Somehow he always managed to have his pristine white shirt tucked into his khaki pants, and this time was no exception.

"Please, I am happy you are here. Sueto will bring us now some coffee." He waved at Sueto and stumbled against the cabinet on the far wall. He yanked open its door and pulled out two bottles of whiskey. Michael and Tom clapped their hands and whistled. Roz and I groaned. Tom jumped up to help the captain get glasses and bottles to the table.

Sueto appeared over my shoulder, holding a tray with a delicate china coffee service. The fishing master followed Sueto, obviously here to join the party. He took the chair beside me.

Gently, Sueto placed cups in front of each of us and set the pot in the middle of the table. "I come back with food next." He hurried from the cabin.

"This is our fishing master, Satomurasan. I don't know if you have met him?" I questioned Michael and gestured toward Satomura. "He's from a beautiful part of Japan, Hokaido."

The fishing master smiled and nodded, understanding only the word Hokaido. Michael grabbed his hand, jerking it up and down, saying loudly, "G'day, Mate. Nice to meet ya." Satomurasan looked startled and stared at his wildly flailing hand, as though it were a foreign object, out of his control. I felt embarrassed for Michael.

The cabin door opened to admit a Japanese man I had never seen before.

"Ah, captain, you made it!" Tom turned to Roz. "He's the captain of the transfer ship."

Our captain and Satomura rose from their seats and bowed to the second captain. Suetosan appeared, dragging another chair into the already crowded room, and placed it at the end of the table.

Tom had set glasses in front of everyone and the captain slopped whiskey into each one. Roz and I covered our glasses to prevent him from filling them. Roz picked up the coffee pot and poured coffee into our cups, politely offering it to the men.

"Mr. Mike, where you from?" The captain propped himself up on one elbow.

Ah, a bit of heaven, captain. That's where I hail from. A wee spot on the north island, called Opunake. It's close to Mt. Egmont—you know our mountain that looks just like a cone." Michael spoke in rapid-fire Kiwi English. I remembered my first interaction with Kazuki on the *Kyowa*, where I had rambled on about finding the bridge. The captain had the same blank look on his face.

"Perhaps if you speak slower, he may be able to understand you." I suggested gently to Mike.

"I think light bulbs from America are best kind in the world." The captain sighed as he spoke. "Light bulbs: L-i-g-h-t-b-u-l-b-s."

Mike looked at me, puzzled. I shrugged, knowing only that the captain was getting drunker and this was just the beginning.

Suetosan returned, carefully balancing a fully laden tray. He unloaded empty plates and chopsticks onto our table, followed by tiny bowls of soy sauce, hot mustard and sesame seeds. Iidasan appeared and tried to maneuver his bulk into the cabin but could not manage to squeeze around my chair, no matter how close I pulled to the table. He gave up and handed his tray of food to Sueto. A large electric frying pan appeared and was placed in the middle of the table.

The captain refilled his whiskey glass and said, "Elephants have largest ears of all animals in the world. Elephants: E-l-e-p-h-a-n-t-s."

I caught Roz's eye and coughed into my napkin, trying to mask my laugh. Sueto squeezed between Mike and me and ducked under the table with the cord from the frying pan in his hand. I felt him crawl over my feet as he searched for the socket. Tom, having been in conversation with Roz, had not noticed Sueto's new position and looked around, puzzled. "Bloody hell, there's something on the floor, having a pull at me feet!" He tried to look under the table, but the tight quarters allowed him no room to maneuver.

Roz patted his hand. "Don't worry, it's just Suetosan."

"What the hell is sway-toes-son?" Tom asked, just as Sueto emerged from the end of the table, standing up and leaning over the captain's shoulder to turn on the electric skillet. He tossed strips of beef and chicken into the pan, as well as curls of chopped cabbage.

Our fishing master and the captain of the transfer ship were engaged in a deep discussion in Japanese. Tom asked Roz where she was from and it turned out to be his hometown, which set them trying to find acquaintances in common. The sizzling sounds of the meat and chicken mingled with the loud conversation.

Mike asked me what part of the States I was from. As I tried to reply, Suetosan thrust his body between the two of us to stir the food, interrupting the flow of conversation. The captain began singing "Tinkle, tinkle, little star . . . I love you wherever you are . . ."

I tried to swallow my mouthful of coffee but couldn't. I spewed it into my cup, struggling to stifle my laughter. I closed my eyes, fighting to maintain control. My body shook all over.

Suddenly the captain blurted out, over the hubbub of the conversation next to him, "Rozsan take many baths!" He reached across Tom with his left arm and grabbed Roz's hand, pulling to it his lips and kissing it loudly. His right elbow plopped into a dish of soy sauce, and a spray of tiny brown spots speckled his white shirt.

I rocked back and forth, gasping with laughter. I clenched my knees together, sure that I was about to wet my pants. My coffee cup crunched onto the table, shattering into dozens of pieces. Roz looked at me and quickly away, her cheeks blowing in and out and her lips quivering uncontrollably.

"Please, you must excuse us." She gasped. "We need to . . . we have to . . ." I tried to speak and a choking sound came from my throat.

"The loo . . . we have to go to the loo!" Roz leapt to her feet, her chair crashing over backwards. I willed my bladder to hold tight and weakly got to my feet, waving and nodding, my lips clamped tightly together. I turned and fled, Roz just behind me.

As I stumbled along the corridor, breathing in jagged gasps, I hissed over my shoulder at Roz, "Stop it, stop it . . . don't make me . . . I have to pee!"

"Light bulbs!! I didn't even know they made light bulbs in America!" She shoved me over the threshold of the toilet room.

Roz latched the door and we let go. Animal-like shrieks. Howls of laughter. Tears ran down my face. I could not breathe. Roz doubled over and slid to the floor.

"His lips . . . I think he was *licking* my hand!" She rubbed her hand on her shirt. "And what about his hair? It looked the best I've seen it in there, dontcha' reckon?

"All I want to know is . . ." I struggled to compose myself. "Did *you* teach him 'Tinkle Tinkle Little Star?'"

They found us there, an hour or so later. Sueto knocked and knocked on the door, until we were forced to open it. He and Iidasan stared at us, two heaps of sodden, tear-stained observers, one leaning against the wall, the other huddled by the toilet. Neither one of them said a word, simply shaking their heads and quietly pulling the door shut as they left us alone.

SEVENTEEN

KGB

BY THE TIME I BOARDED THE *IVAN MALYKIN* IN WELLINGTON ON December 9, 1988, I had worked on four Soviet ships for a total of seven months, both in Alaska and New Zealand. My feelings for the Soviets ran like a river, twisting and turning, rarely clear on their course. I felt my emotions paralleled their lives, where nothing is straightforward and everything is full of conflict.

I loathed the Soviet political system. My sparkling balloon of idealism had burst during my time at sea, where I lived in a world that forced human beings to give up their dignity and adulthood. The strength of my hatred was new for me; I didn't know what to do with it. I sometimes thought that I should stop working with the Soviets, go back to my Japanese boats. Work under a system more like my own, seek out relief from the hard-edged bitterness that sat like a rock in my chest. Work with people where a barrier to intimacy kept me from losing myself in their world and their lives. But the Soviets were like an addiction for me; I could not seem to escape them. Their passions matched mine in intensity, something I had rarely found in my search for kindred souls. I was drawn in by their love and affection, like I was on the losing end of the rope in tug-of-war. The memories I took from each person who shared her or his life with me became an intricate part of me and of how I viewed the world.

With this mix of emotions I boarded the *Ivan Malykin*. Roz, from the *Akagi Maru*, was off on another Japanese boat, and my Kiwi coworker was a woman named Carol Sutherland. I knew her only slightly from our orientation session, and this was the first time that we had worked together. Carol seemed to have a good sense of humor. Humor was the one weapon, so far, that helped me manage my anger when it threatened to take over. Carol was also a veteran of Soviet ships. We had spent a couple of days together at MAF, trading experiences and thoughts on the Soviets. She had feelings like mine—though she hated the Soviet system, she loved the people—which is why she kept coming back, as I did. For both of us, what we gained outweighed the frustrations.

The *Malykin* had been docked in Wellington for a couple of days by the time Carol and I reported for duty. Boardings in New Zealand were completely different from those in Alaska. We actually met the boats in port instead of making death-defying transfers at sea. I lived in Wellington, so I simply took a taxi down to the dock to meet Carol and find the *Malykin*. MAF had sent our gear over to the boat earlier that morning.

I loved the docks. Big ships from all over the world surrounded me as I walked along the length of the concrete pier, searching for the familiar sight of a rust-covered, peeling gray hull, the hammer and sickle painted on a red smokestack. I tried to pronounce the strange names painted on the sterns of the vessels. I stopped to look at a blue and white star-filled flag, flapping from the stern of a massive red cargo ship, wondering from what far-flung country this boat had sailed. A sense of adventure filled me when I spotted Carol waving from the end of the dock. I picked up my pace and grinned happily as I joined her in front of the *Malykin*. Cranes and cables clanked around us as cargo was unloaded from ships; the voices of men shouting orders to each other filled the air.

Carol looked at me and winked. "Well, here we go!" I followed her up the gangplank that led from the dock to the boat, gripping the ropes strung as hand rails for balance as we dipped and swayed our way to the top. We stepped onto the deck of the *Malykin* and a baby-faced man introduced himself as Igor, the watch officer.

"Please you to stay here. I find commissar. OK?" He looked at us nervously.

"*Horasho. Speciba.*" I smiled and thanked him. He grinned awkwardly at me and turned, nearly tripping over himself in his haste to fetch the commissar.

The deck loomed silently in front of us. The requisite rusty barrels and ungainly stacks of tattered netting covered much of its surface. All the crew members of the *Malykin* were off in Wellington, leaving the ship as quiet as a ghost town. Before they docked, the commissar assigned every ship member to a group, with a "trusted comrade" in charge of each group. What the group got to do all depended on the comrade—some allowed their groups only to window shop, others allowed their groups to bar hop.

The commissar allowed each group a two-to-four hour period off the ship. At the end of their allotted time, they had to report back. If everyone appeared in good shape and there were no problems, the group could go off again for a second couple of hours. The group leader had strict orders to keep everyone together at all times—no one was to venture off on their own. If one person had to go to the bathroom, they all went. I had lived this over and over again, going around with my Soviet friends in their tightly regulated groups. I always felt guilty when, unable to cope any longer with these restrictions, I would wave good-bye to my friends and set off on my own, knowing envious Soviet eyes followed me as I made my escape.

Before they left for their outing, the commissar gave each crew member a N.Z. $20 advance against their salary. It was illegal for crew members to have their own money while at sea and salaries were paid at the end of the voyage. So, theoretically, this N.Z. $20 was all the money they had, which meant little danger of a crew member defecting while on their tourist outing. After all, how far could they get on $20? If a commissar did his job properly, on boarding before leaving the Soviet Union, he searched every crew member's personal belongings and did a body search to ensure that no one had hard currency or alcohol with them.

I had learned about the black market on most vessels. Anything was available for a price—hard currency and alcohol especially. Sometimes crew members would bribe a corrupt commissar, and he would turn a blind eye to what they brought on board. Those in the network found hiding places on the ship for illegal cash and alcohol. Later in the cruise, these items were sold or bartered among the crew. Risk-taking entrepreneurs did well for themselves. This underground system virtually ran every ship.

Carol pulled me away from the deck railing as Igor returned with a well-dressed, strikingly attractive man. His tight, short sleeved knit shirt showed off his well defined body. He introduced himself to us as Evgeny, the commissar. Smooth features lay over a flawless, sun tanned face. When he smiled, his teeth were all perfectly white, without even a hint of metal. His icy blue eyes were not involved in his smile.

My first thought about Evgeny was that he must rank high within the Communist party, as only the elite had access to good dental care. I had learned to try and size up the commissar as quickly as possible; he, alone, set the tone for the boat. Experience had taught me to trust my instinct. My instant reaction to this man was one of distrust. His surface was polished, smiling and welcoming, but without warmth. Underneath I sensed cruelty and manipulation. I was sure he put his unusual good looks to use for the latter. Evgeny's eyes gleamed with intelligence. This man was not stupid, as some of my past commissars had been, which made him all the more dangerous.

"Welcome to the *Ivan Malykin*. Please, I will show you to your cabin. I trust that you are looking forward to your journey with us. We have an all new crew on the *Malykin*; they were flown down a week ago. The last crew went home for much needed rest." Evgeny spoke accented, excellent English. Another clue indicating his position; very few Soviets spoke English of this caliber.

Carol and I followed Evgeny to the cabin which we would share. The *Malykin* was a Kamchatka boat, as had been the *Orekhova*, so I knew the lay out of the ship. I felt at home as we stepped into the living quarters and the familiar and indescribable Soviet ship odor immediately enveloped me. The observer cabin was on the port side of the deck level, just as mine had been on the *Orekhova*.

Evgeny ushered us into our cabin. Our gear was stacked neatly in one corner, and Evgeny said our baskets were in the factory. On the table in the middle of the room, he pointed to some printed propaganda and told us he hoped this information would be interesting to us. I had been deluged with this stuff on other boats; it consisted of photographic pamphlets of happy, well fed Soviets working in factories or in the fields. Though the text was in Russian, previous commissars had explained its message to me at great length.

Evgeny looked at his watch. Good Lord—it looked like a Rolex. Where would he have gotten a watch that cost more than most Soviets made in a year? I was becoming more and more worried about this man.

"It is now 3 p.m. I will leave you to unpack and then, if you wish, in half an hour you may meet me on the bridge for a tour of the ship. Is this agreeable to you?" Evgeny looked at us questioningly. "Do you know how to find the bridge?"

"Yes, thank you. We will meet you in half an hour. I have worked on several Kamchatka boats, so we can easily find the bridge." I smiled politely. Evgeny seemed to bow slightly, then he turned and left, shutting the door behind him.

Carol collapsed on the couch that ran along the wall beneath the porthole. I raised my eyebrows and looked at her. She tapped her watch and held up two fingers. We waited about two minutes in silence, then I opened the cabin door and looked into the corridor, scanning its length for any sign of life.

I shoved the door shut and announced, "Empty!"

"Bloody Hell, just our luck to get stuck with a Big One for our commissar." Carol rolled her eyes. "Where did this bloke come from?"

"Did you see his watch? Could it possibly have been a real Rolex? Do you know how much those cost?" I still could not get over this.

"You know what I think?" Carol said. "I think he's KGB. And I think he is going to be a bloody problem."

"God, you might be right. The little bit we've seen sure tells me our friend is no normal commissar. I mean, the ones I've worked with have never been *this* slick." I shook my head worriedly.

Carol jumped up, shaking herself brusquely, as if to rid her body of the evil presence of Evgeny. "I think I'll do a loo check. Do ya think this one will be as bad as they usually are?" We laughed together, easing the tension.

I began unpacking, opting for the top bunk. Two of us, plus all of our gear, were going to be tight in this cabin. MAF generously gave each observer a supplemental food allotment, of which both Carol and I had taken advantage. There were stacked cartons of canned fruit, soft drinks, cookies (biscuits, as we called them in New Zealand) and chocolate that the stevedore had delivered. Definitely cushier than being an observer in the Bering Sea.

The door flew open and Carol burst into the room, bringing the faint, familiar toilet odor with her. "Just as bad as they always are. I do hope they've given us some bloody strong soap." She stepped to the cabin's sink and picked up the soap from its perch, sniffing it. "This'll do." She scrubbed vigorously and jerked on the faucet, leaping sideways to avoid the first gush of rusty water, which splashed out onto the floor, spreading like a bloodstain across the dirty gray linoleum.

After Carol cleaned up as best she could, we headed off to the bridge and the commissar. Evgeny gave us a routine tour of the boat, with an added surprise. He actually took us down to the factory, something I had never had a commissar do. Factories were for the workers or the factory manager. He was very solicitous and wanted to make sure that we had everything we needed to do our work. As per usual, he did not show us the crew's quarters. He did, however, show us the crew's mess, and he invited us to attend the nightly movies that he would be showing. He told us when meals were served, and showed us where his cabin was, insisting that if we needed anything at all, we should come to him immediately. He was definitely a smooth one.

I asked what time we were due to sail, and Evgeny said 8 p.m. Carol and I decided to head into town, a five-minute walk away, and do some last-minute shopping. Evgeny instructed us to be back by 6 p.m.

The Soviets were easy to spot in town. Not only did their tight-knit groups give them away, but also their clothing. The men were dressed in their best, which usually meant a cheap brown or gray polyester suit, mustard colored tie and scruffy, worn shoes of imitation leather. No one's clothes ever seemed to fit properly. I could never decide if this was because the men gained and lost weight at sea or the clothes were of such poor quality that they would look awkward no matter what. Probably a bit of both.

As I wandered anonymously along the sidewalk, I watched the Soviets try desperately to look as if they belonged in the hustle and bustle of downtown Wellington, but no attempts could succeed. A casual saunter turned into a nervous glance over the shoulder; was the commissar or one of his spuins following? Nonchalance at storefront window displays quickly changed to slack-jawed amazement as they gazed at items that, until this moment, had existed only in their dreams. Their wonder as they looked at goods they had never seen before—and could never afford to own— saddened me. Their faces contained a mixture of amazement, eagerness, and innocence. I felt a strange pang of sorrow for these people, while studying them from a distance, as though framed in a photograph. For now, I stood apart. Soon, however, I would be among them. Like a captured insect cocooned by a spider, I would be wrapped up in the Soviets, drawn into their lives. I smiled, wondering what lay ahead.

EIGHTEEN

New Year's Eve

CAROL AND I RETURNED TO THE SHIP AT 6 P.M., PER EVGENY'S instructions. All evening, solemn men in dark suits hurried on and off the vessel, usually with Evgeny in tow. They walked with their heads bent together, whispering agitatedly to each other. One suit was more animated than the others, and he swung his arms wildly while I watched as he and Evgeny stood near the top of the gangplank. I thought he would push Evgeny over the side. Unlike the self-assured Evgeny who had greeted us when we boarded the *Malykin*, this one stood with head bowed and shoulders slumped, a posture of defeat.

Around 8 p.m., Carol and I strolled to the officer's dining room. We had decided the men in suits were from the Soviet Embassy in Wellington. But what had happened that had them so upset? We entered the dining room to find the captain and chief mate hunched over their plates, looking miserable. Both managed a strained greeting as we said, "*Pretna apetitia*," and sat down to join them. Politely, the captain asked if we found our accommodation suitable.

"Yes, thank you. And Evgeny has been very helpful." I smiled at him.

The captain cleared his throat and said that Evgeny was busy with preparations for leaving so would not join us for dinner. The radio officer stood abruptly and said, "*Pretna apetitia*," nodding at the captain to join him. The two left quickly.

"What is going on?" Carol and I shrugged at each other.

Suddenly, a heavy set woman with shoulder length auburn

hair charged around the corner, stopping abruptly when she saw us. We nodded and smiled at her, introducing ourselves. She grinned at us and told us her name was Lucy, and she would get our food for us.

Lucy disappeared into her serving room and quickly bustled back to our table with bowls of steaming borscht. She stood over us as we sampled the soup and told her it was delicious. Her soft face crinkled into another grin that stopped suddenly, as if she had remembered something unpleasant. She sighed and sank down into the chair beside Carol. She looked at us worriedly, her brown eyes large and round.

"Lucy, what is wrong? Are you alright?" I asked with concern.

"Today, in Wellington is big problem." Her eyes were huge. "One crewman try to leave ship. He try to stay in New Zealand!"

A defection—this was big news! No wonder Evgeny had looked defeated when I saw him on deck with the Embassy official—a defection was the ultimate nightmare of every commissar. Lucy told us the defector's name was Sergei and he was the assistant radio officer. Men from the Embassy had taken him away.

"I only know that now it will to be very hard on all of us. Commissar is very angry." Immediately after divulging this information, she threw her apron over her face, slowly and dramatically pulling it down to peer at us over its edge.

"Please, you must not say to anyone I tell you this. Officers think we do not know about Sergei." She rolled her eyes at the stupidity of the officers, sighing and leaning back in her chair, relieved to be unburdened of her secret. We assured Lucy we wouldn't tell anyone. Thanking her for the borscht, we left the dining room.

"This place is like a bloody tomb." Carol commented as we walked the empty corridors. "Everyone is likely laying low due to the trouble. Let's take a spin onto the deck—might be good time to check out the bins without the crew mucking about."

We made our way out to the deck, seeing and hearing no one. Floodlights from the dock illuminated the *Malykin*, and we scrambled over nets, lines, and cables to reach the fish bins. They were positioned on the stern and port sides of the ship and looked the same size as those on the *Orekhova*. As we walked back toward the middle of the deck, a hissing sound darted at us from the darkness. Shielding my eyes from the glare of the floodlights, I spotted a head poking out of a small room in the center of the deck, tucked up against the wall between the two entry way doors. The head was followed by a hand waving us over.

We zigzagged to the small room and arrived in front of a smiling man who greeted us with, "*Dobre Viecher*. Please, come in with us." With a flourish, he bowed as we stepped into the tiny, box-like room. This was obviously the *Malykin's* chi room. There were benches against the walls, a small table in the middle of the floor and a teapot and hot plate on a corner shelf. Two men grinned at us from the benches, moving over to make room for us to sit down.

Our greeter sat down beside me and we smiled at each other. This man's face was full of character and a life lived deeply, and perhaps not easily. Laugh lines crinkled around his dark brown eyes. Two dimples appeared in his cheeks. Our smiles grew bigger as we shook hands. A warm feeling washed over me, coupled with a strange sense of familiarity. I felt as if I knew this man from somewhere, as if we were long-time friends. A memory rose in my mind of a family reunion, where I met a cousin I had never seen before. An electric jolt of familiarity shocked me as I realized that we looked alike. I did not know her, but I felt strongly connected to her. Valerya did not look like me. And I did not know him. But I felt it—this instant familiarity—stretched like a cord between us, connecting us in an invisible way that I had no words for.

He said, "I know you are Dasha because you are the big one. I am Valerya, trawl chief. These two of my crew." Valerya reached to shake Carol's hand, calling her by her Russian name, Cotick.

Carol had placed herself between two men who introduced themselves as Sergei and Viktor. Looking at Viktor for really the first time, my eyes widened with unease. If he had worn an eye patch, he could have passed as Blackbeard's brother. His swarthy dark looks and scruffy black hair, combined with his crooked grin and missing front tooth, gave him a menacing appearance. In direct contrast, Sergei's liquid brown eyes gazed at me as yearningly as a new puppy. His face—indeed his whole body—was chubby and soft and his smile full and eager.

Despite the somber atmosphere on the ship, the three men were cheerful and laughing and very glad to see us. Carol and I slipped quickly into the immediate camaraderie that we had come to expect of the Soviets.

"Are there only three of you on this crew?" I asked Valerya.

"Oh, no—two more, another Sergei and Nikolai. Together we are Trawl Band-o."

I could not resist. "No, I think you are not Trawl Band-o—I think you are Trawl *Banditos!*"

Even the Soviets understood the seemingly universal word "banditos," and the men burst into laughter.

"Banditos! Banditos? You think we are banditos?!" Viktor pulled a bandanna up over his face and Sergei found a wool hat and pulled it low over his eyes. "Now maybe we are real banditos!"

So that is how the nickname for our favorite deck crew came about. From then on, these men were the Trawl Banditos, usually just "The Banditos" for short. Carol and I both had a passion for nicknames, and eventually everyone of importance got one. Sergei, who was working hard to learn English, could never understand the difference between shoe, slipper, and sandal. Therefore he was christened "Mr. Slipper." Viktor constantly tried to impress us with his strength and what he thought was a perfect physique, so, to torment him, we called him "Bulichka," a Russian puff pastry. Next to Carol, I seemed like an Amazon to the men, so my name was "Big D." To match me, Valerya became "Big V." Carol was "Malinky C"—Little C.

At one point, Sergei said something about the "problem" that had occurred, and the mood turned somber. There was a heated discussion in Russian among the three men, of which I could only follow a bit. The gist seemed to be how foolish the defector had been and how it was going to be very bad for him now. Valerya told us that the assistant radio operator, Sergei, had run from his group in Wellington and turned up at the city police station. The speculation was that he had spotted the police station while jaunting around town, as it was in a central location. None of the men seemed to think that he had a local contact; it appeared as if he had acted on his own. The police called the Soviet Embassy, and, as far as anyone knew Sergei was in their hands.

I could only speculate at the politics of a situation like this. If Sergei really wanted asylum in New Zealand, surely the liberal Labour government would consider his case on a human rights basis. And because he was a radio operator, who knew what kind of useful political information he held? On the other hand, the Ministry of Agriculture and Fisheries lived in fear of something like this happening. Soviet fishing was a lucrative business for the Kiwis, and if, by granting the defector asylum, they enraged the Soviets enough to leave New Zealand, it would be an enormous blow to the industry. We heard rumors later that Sergei was sent back to the Soviet Union and never got a chance to present his case.

Just before midnight, the chief mate stuck his head in the chi room and said the men were needed on deck. We were ready to cast off.

Before he exited, Valerya said, "Always you must come here when not working. This room is our home—all of us together. We will drink tea, talk. Even make *kartoshkas!*" With this, he winked at me, because I had made it known earlier that fried *kartoshkas* were one of my favorite treats.

I went up to the flying bridge to watch as the Malykin left the dock. I had a glorious view of the night time skyline of Wellington. Lights danced far up into the hills that surrounded the city. I breathed deeply of the urban smell, trying to capture its essence before we left it behind. Sometimes I missed it, in those months at sea. I thought of Valerya. My attraction to him had been instant, without question. But it was not sexual. I tried to put a name on my strong feelings for him. It seemed important to categorize them, to fit them neatly into my internal list of emotions one can have for another person. But they would not fit into a labeled column, easily listed and defined. Later, much later, I would understand why.

*   *   *

For the next several days, the mood on the ship was tense. The commissar had long, closed-door meetings with the crew in the crew's mess. He also called each person individually to his cabin. Some people he met with for a long time—others only a few minutes. The Banditos told us that he was trying to find out if anyone had assisted Sergei with his escape. He offered "rewards" to those who might come forward with information on their fellow crew members. It was during this process that the commissar's two main informants were identified: Eura, a helmsman who worked on the bridge from 4-8 p.m. and Sasha, who would be working in the fish meal plant when we began fishing. Since this crew was an all new one, no one had known who the spies were. In addition to calling them "spuins," the Soviets used the term slugs, which I thought extremely appropriate. The slugs had no friends among the crew and were completely ostracized. I would catch myself feeling sorry for them when I glimpsed them sitting alone in the crew's mess—I had to remind myself of the role they had chosen to keep these feelings of sympathy at bay.

We reached the fishing grounds in two days. When work began, the atmosphere on the *Malykin* normalized somewhat. People had work to focus on now, not just constant speculation about Sergei and his defection. But the commissar seemed to have eyes and ears everywhere. When Carol and I saw him at mealtimes, he often commented on our activities, noting where we had been and with whom. There was nothing threatening or even reproaching in his words. It was as if he simply wanted us to know that he was always aware of our whereabouts.

"Bloody Hell, that prick must have more than just the two slugs. He knows our every move!" Carol couldn't believe it and neither could I.

I often stayed behind after meals in the dining room and talked with Lucy, our server, who quickly became my key to the *Malykin* grapevine. She told me that whenever she spoke with Carol or me, the commissar would question her afterward about what we had discussed.

"Dasha, every day commissar come to me and say 'Lucy, what observers say to you?' He will come here today, after you leave." She angrily clanked the dishes together as she stacked them.

"Lucy, maybe I should not stay and speak with you after our eating."

She puffed out her lips angrily. "Why not? What is wrong with our speaking here together? Commissar is . . ." she rolled her finger around her ear in the universal sign for crazy.

I had a wild thought about his intense interest in us. I broached it to Carol.

"Carol—what about this one: Do you think Evgeny thinks *we* were somehow involved in Sergei's defection?"

Carol's eyes widened. "Could be. Could be. But then again—this was a whole new crew, so when would we have had a chance to meet this guy? The pillock must realize we didn't even know Sergei." Carol was right. I chalked up the commissar's obsession with us as just part of his being a shrewd and diligent commissar who was probably trying to save his career.

The *Malykin* was fishing for black dory, a scaly, spiny fish with delectable white flesh. Unlike many of my Soviet ships, the *Malykin* trawled 24 hours a day. Carol and I worked 12-hour shifts so that we could sample every trawl. Like Roz, Carol was a night owl and preferred to work 6 p.m. to 6 a.m. and sleep during the day. I was able to keep to a normal schedule. We each slept with earplugs so our respective comings and goings would not disturb the other.

Despite the constant shadow of the commissar, Valerya and the Banditos were adamant that we spend time with them in the chi room. If I didn't show up after work, I learned to expect the sound of Mr. Slipper padding down the corridor to our cabin. His head would poke around the corner and those eager puppy eyes would reproach me.

"Dasha, the Banditos wait for you. Why you not with us?"

What a feeling, to be so sought after. I wondered if this was what it felt like to be the High School Homecoming Queen. Grinning with happiness, I would gather up my paperwork and follow Mr. Slipper out to join my friends in the chi room. Carol had set up her tape player and we played all sorts of music, from Russian classical to reggae. One evening I brought out a stash of biscuits and chocolate to add to the tea collection, and all of the Banditos belonged to us forever. Any kind of decent sweet was hard to come by on the ships.

Valerya and I spent many hours together in the chi room. I wanted to know him, to learn all about him. He told me about his life at home in Moscow, speaking of his wife and daughter, whom he missed terribly. The three of them and his 78-year old mother lived together in a two bedroom flat which had been passed on to Nina, Valeyra's wife, from her mother. Her mother had gone to live with another daughter. I knew decent housing was in short supply in Russia. Valerya was fortunate to have a two bedroom flat—often families lived in only one or two rooms.

I told Valerya I wanted to go to Africa and see the animals there. This had been my dream since I was a young child and first saw photographs of these magnificent creatures. Valerya could not fathom why I wanted to go to Africa. He was convinced that I would be eaten alive by lions or leopards. He was shaking his head in disbelief when Slipper and Bulichka walked into the chi room. He recounted my wish to them and they, too, stared at me as though I must be out of my mind.

"Dasha, in south of Kazakstan, a wild tiger came into two towns and killed many people. When the children walked to school, the tiger waited in the bush and attacked them. He ate much meat from these children. Finally, some men in the town shot and killed this tiger. When you go to Africa, will you have gun?" Valerya questioned me. I told him that I would not be able to travel with a gun, and his concerned face slipped into a frown.

"What you to do, Dasha, when a wild lion comes to eat you if you have no gun? I do not like this at all. I think it is best if you go to the zoo in America to see these animals. Safe this way." Valerya's mind was made up.

One day, Valerya announced that he wanted to learn to knit. Carol had taught me the basics of knitting, and she and I would often knit away as we sat with the Banditos. Valerya decided this activity looked similar to net-mending, so he thought he would be a natural.

Carol loaned him her knitting needles and the lesson began. His large, callused hands gripped the long, white needles tightly, reminding me of how I had grasped my chopsticks that first time on the *Kyowa*. Valerya was missing the little finger of his left hand as well as the tip of the third finger on the same hand. Despite this, his fingers turned and twisted with an agility that surprised me. Soon he had a completed strip of soft, white New Zealand wool, as I still struggled to finish a single row. He grinned happily at me.

"Big D, this will be surprise for you." I wondered what he had in mind. A few days later, he proudly presented me with a tiny, perfect white scarf. From behind his back he pulled my small stuffed bear that was my lucky charm and accompanied me on all of my boats. Carefully, he tied the scarf around the bear's neck, finishing it off with a small bow. To this day, I still have my good luck bear and it still wears this scarf.

Several weeks into the cruise, I worked around the clock one night because Carol did not feel well and needed sleep. A small trawl of black dory filled my time from 10 p.m. until shortly after midnight. I stayed behind in the factory, after the crew men left, to do some extra length frequencies. The empty factory felt like another world. Subtle sounds filtered into my consciousness, sounds that were usually buried by the cacophony of noise that normally dominated this work area. A soft clanking from the starboard side of the conveyors. Water trickled from a hose near my feet. The whoosh of the ocean through the sluice doors that opened directly onto the sea. I walked over to the sluice door and lay down on my stomach, my raingear protecting me from the damp and slime on the factory floor. I pulled off my rubber glove and stuck my bare hand out, into the sea. The cold water washed over my arm, up to my elbow. I had been on the ocean for months, enclosed in these strong steel barriers that separated us. Except for the time the wave poured through my porthole on the *Akagi*, I had never touched the sea from one of my boats.

The stillness from the factory seemed to follow me as I made my way up to the deck. Stacks of nets and dark, silent barrels loomed in the blackness. No one walked on the deck, or hung over the railing, smoking and whispering. I stopped in the safe cocoon of the night and leaned on the railing, watching the ocean rush below me. The churning wake glowed an eerie green, illuminated by tiny bits of phosphorescence. I breathed deeply as the wind rushed against my face. The stars glowed like pinpoints above me. I felt alone. And I missed my world. I had been in New Zealand for over a year and working on these boats longer than that. I wanted to be with people who understood me, in a culture that was my own. I missed my friends in Seattle. I longed for, it seemed, a little bit of everything that I had left behind in the states.

I looked forward and saw only a single light glowing on the darkened deck, the light in the chi room. I plodded over and poked my head in the door. Valerya sat, alone, drinking tea.

His smile washed over me. "Dasha, *sadis!*" He patted the bench across from him. "Here, some chi for you. You have been working too much." He stirred sweetened milk into a mug of tea and handed it to me, his face full of affection.

I sighed and sat down, thinking of how much I loved this man. So much separated us, but so much drew us together. What would it be like if things were different?

"Dasha, you seem sad tonight. What is wrong for you?" He looked at me intently.

"Ah, Valerya, tonight I am sad. I miss my friends. I miss my life at home. What I love most feels very far away right now."

"You know, Dasha, in my language, we call this *rodynya*. I cannot translate this exactly for you, but it means you love your country because it is your home."

"Valerya, do you love your country?" I had never asked a Soviet this question.

Valerya was silent for a long moment. Then, softly, he said "*Da*, I do."

"How can you, when your country makes your life so hard? How can you love something that treats you so badly?" I could feel my anger swell, a balloon inflating.

"*Rodynya*, Dasha. It means that, no matter what, this love of your home is bigger than any other love. Maybe I do not love what my government does," Valerya lowered his voice. "But Russia is my home."

My voice was barely a whisper. "If you could come and live in the United States, or New Zealand, would you do it?"

"Ah, Dasha, I believe only a strong or foolish person would leave his home and go to a country where he is a stranger. I hope I am not a fool. And I know that I am not strong in the way that I would have to be."

I argued with him, of course. I saw his strength every day. In the way he treated his crew, with dignity and fairness. In the way they responded to him, with respect and admiration. In the way he quietly refused to bend to the commissar. In the kindness he showed all of us around him. Valerya could not be convinced that he carried within him the strength to start a new life. But I knew he did.

*   *   *

As New Year's approached, our excitement built. This would be my second Christmas and New Year's on a Soviet ship. Christmas, of course, was not a holiday for the Soviets because of its Christian origins. Interestingly enough, many of what I knew as Christmas customs, the Soviets incorporated into their New Year festivities. There were "*yulkas*"—Christmas trees. And "*Det Moros*"—Santa Claus. On New Year's Eve, *Det Moros* made his appearance. Gifts were exchanged on New Year's Day. Decorations were put up—streamers and banners—a few days before the New Year. On my Soviet ship last year, the commissar had been a low-key type, and we had a huge party and dance in the crew's mess that went on until all hours. Alcohol was definitely in evidence, and the commissar had turned a blind eye. I wondered what type of celebration Evgeny would allow his crew members this year.

While in Wellington, Carol and I had loaded on a small, artificial Christmas tree. Just before Christmas, we set it up in our cabin and festooned it with decorations we had brought with us. We strung decorations up in the chi room as well. Lucy invited us to help her and the other two women crew members decorate the *yulkas* in the crew's mess and the officer's dining room. The entire ship took on a very festive air and spirits ran high as the holiday approached.

A few days before New Year's Eve, the commissar called an all ship meeting (excepting observers) to announce what the festivities would be for the crew. We got the scoop from the Banditos later in the chi room.

"Will we get to have a dance party?" I excitedly asked the men. Carol had pre-empted me on the details, getting them from the chief mate, with whom she had become friendly, and said, "Bloody Hell, no way—listen to what his idea of a good time is."

Valerya proceeded to describe the commissar's plan for the New Year's celebration. The cook had been ordered to make a large fruit pie and the crew would gather in the crew's mess at 9 p.m. on New Year's Eve. There, they would eat pie and drink milk and the commissar would offer a New Year's toast. After eating their pie, all crew members were to go back to their individual cabins.

I laughed in disbelief. "That's it? That is how you are going to celebrate the New Year?"

Valerya assured me that was not all the *Banditos* were going to do to see in the New Year, and we were invited to come to his and Mr. Slipper's cabin around 11 p.m. on New Year's Eve.

On New Year's Eve day, Carol said to me "I'm afraid I've gotten us into a bit of a pinch. I promised starpom (the chief mate) that we would come to his cabin tonight for a party with him and the captain and some of the others. He has this idea that he wants all of the women on the ship to help him see in the New Year. Since you and me make up two of the five, I couldn't very well refuse him, now could I?"

Carol and I got on well with the chief mate and the captain. More importantly, they both detested the commissar, which endeared them to us even more. I told Carol not to worry—we would let the Banditos know that we would be late but would come to their cabin as soon as we could gracefully get away from starpom.

Around 9 that evening, Carol and I both crept over to the crew's mess and peered surreptitiously through the crack in the closed door. Sure enough, the commissar and his two slugs were serving up pie to the few crew members that had come to the "celebration." There were only about a dozen people in attendance. We watched as the commissar bade everyone be seated and launched into some sort of spiel about strength to resist temptation and the proper way to start off a new year with healthy food and drink. Carol and I both rolled our eyes at each other and tiptoed back to our cabin.

At 10 p.m., we arrived, dressed in our best, at the starpom's cabin. "Our best" was nothing compared to what the other three women wore. Lucy was decked out in a beautiful red shimmery dress with gold earrings and a gold necklace. She looked dazzling. The other two women, Julia and Ilga, were resplendent in green and gold dresses. Julia's was an off-the-shoulder gown that showed off her svelte figure. She was seated next to the starpom. The captain was there, as well as the radio officer. The captain motioned eagerly for us to sit beside him, patting the two chairs on his left. I eased into my seat, marveling at the heavily laden table. What a feast— the usual wonderful Soviet delicacies of caviar, pickles, salads, meats and patés. We laughed and toasted each other with Kamchatka mineral water. Shortly before midnight, the starpom pulled out several bottles of vodka and champagne and proposed that we now start the *real* toasts. Just as he popped the champagne cork, the door flew open and the commissar stepped in. He glared first at us then at the bottles of alcohol and said, in English, "Bad business." Turning, he left the room.

"These blokes are bloody *officers*!" Carol was livid. "I can't believe that prick just barged right in to the chief mate's cabin!"

The table had erupted into excited talk, with much hand waving and agitation. I decided to make my exit now, and grabbed Carol to come with me. Everyone was too upset to try hard to detain us. We left without even a "Happy New Year" having been spoken among us.

Back in our cabin, we both flopped down on the couch in dejection. Some New Year's this was turning out to be. We didn't dare go down to Valerya's cabin, as the commissar was obviously on the prowl. A soft knock sounded on our door.

"If it's that bloody commissar, I'll kill him!" Carol hissed as she rushed over to the door, and yanked it open, ready to do battle. Her anger melted when she saw that it was not the commissar but Valerya. He asked why we were not down in his cabin. Carol explained what had happened and we both smiled sadly.

"Sorry to miss the Banditos party." I looked at him wistfully.

"Big D, what are you saying? You must come now to our party. We are waiting for both of you. Please, this way." Valerya motioned for us to follow him. We both protested that it was too dangerous, but Valerya would not listen to us.

We took the back stairs down to the crew's cabins and saw Mr. Slipper peering out of his cabin doorway. His face lit up when he saw us. Quickly, we ducked into the cabin, joining him and Bulichka. A couple of men from the other deck crew were there as well. With our arrival, the tiny cabin was packed. Carol and I were given the seat of honor—Valerya's bottom bunk. The small table in the middle of the room was covered with a less elegant version of the food at the starpom's party. Before we could partake, however, Carol and I had to recite the details of the fiasco in the starpom's cabin. When we finished our tale, the men cursed among themselves. I had picked up even more choice words in my time on the ships, and the worst ones were in full use tonight.

Valerya banged on the table, reminding us that we were here to celebrate the New Year. Mr. Slipper poured mineral water all around, and Valerya raised a toast—the first one of the New Year to our friendship.

Valerya spoke again. "Next toast is to Dasha, my good American friend I love very much. I think we must all enjoy her company while she is on *Malykin* with us, because soon she will go to Africa and we will never see her again after she is eaten by lions!" The cabin filled with laughter. I bounced a peanut off of Valerya's nose.

Bulichka pulled back the curtain to the top bunk, revealing Carol's tape player. He popped in a cassette and turned the volume up high. Russian rock and roll filled the cabin. Seemingly undaunted by the earlier story we had told them, the Banditos pulled out bottles of cherry brandy and vodka.

With exquisite timing, the commissar threw open the door and stepped into the cabin just as the party was getting into full swing. Carol and I both froze. Everyone stopped talking. Someone turned the music down.

The commissar's searching eyes missed nothing in the tiny cabin. I knew he was registering who was there and what bottles were on the table. He locked eyes with Valerya and neither said anything for a full minute. With his usual calm manner, Valerya simply held the commissar's gaze and finally said, "Happy New Year." Through tight lips, the commissar replied with the same words and left the cabin. I felt the sweat rolling down my chest, and my face burned.

"There's going to be bloody hell to pay." Carol moaned.

The men engaged in an intense discussion. What should we do now? The damage was done, so why not continue with our party? Things, it seemed, could not get any worse. Bulichka turned the music back up to full blast and asked me to dance. We careened around the cabin, bumping into everything and everyone. I traded with Carol, and she and Bulichka tried to do a tango and ended up heaped on top of each other in the corner, laughing uncontrollably. When she recovered, we both pulled all of the guys to their feet and led a Conga line round and round the cabin until we were all dizzy. We danced wildly, frenziedly, releasing weeks of pent up frustration. Always, in the back of my mind, was the small, curled up bit of knowledge that when I said good-bye to these men, I would never see them again. I had done it, many times over now. And it never got easier. You would think I would have developed a shell, a protection against the pain of leaving. But building a wall to keep out the Soviets would be like sandbagging the shores of the Outer Banks to stop the ocean. It would never work, at least not for me. Once again, I had lost my heart to these people. And so, on this New Year's Eve, I celebrated. Life and love and what makes us human. The rich joy of a connection so deep and full and so absolutely unexplainable to anyone not of my world.

NINETEEN

Valerya

CAROL WAS RIGHT. THERE WAS HELL TO PAY FOR OUR NEW YEAR'S celebrations. Repercussions shook the ship. The chief mate and captain both were severely reprimanded by the commissar. The chief mate told Carol that what upset Evgeny more than the alcohol itself was the fact that Lucy, Julia and Ilga had been in his cabin imbibing with him. It was that old dichotomy that officers were allowed to drink but not regular crew members. "Too much like children to be allowed alcohol," I recalled the words of my first commissar.

As punishment for the three women, the commissar told them that at the next port call, they would not be allowed ashore. It seemed that he could not restrict the officers' behavior in this way, but the chief mate said that both he and the captain would not be allowed to be group leaders at the next port call. The commissar's slugs would be put in charge of groups and he and the captain would be allowed off the ship only as members, not leaders, of their groups, since it was clear to the commissar that they were no longer to be trusted.

Evgeny meted out the same penalty to the Banditos—no shore leave for them at the next port call. Valerya and Mr. Slipper shrugged this off, but the news hit Bulichka and the others quite hard. I knew how important shore leave was. Everyone was stir crazy after a month or so at sea, and even a few days of being on land was a coveted reward. Simply being able to visit the shops, purchase an ice cream or coke, and wander the streets of town was a rare delight for these people. To have this taken from them, like children punished for a naughty prank, was, indeed, a severe punishment. The commissar had chosen well.

I stepped outside of myself to study what I felt. I thought of the many months it had taken me to reach this point, this place where I no longer allowed my anger at the injustices I lived with to devour me. I did not know if I should count this as a victory or a failure. I only knew that, for me, it was a matter of survival. My painful struggle had taught me that, to live with the system, I had to accept its rules, because they were as inflexible as the steel hulls of the ships on which I sailed.

The only mention Evgeny made to Carol and me of that night was the fact that it was strictly forbidden for the crew to drink alcohol. He needed to maintain strict order and discipline on his boat, otherwise the crew would not work hard. Alcohol did not help his crew to work hard and be good, productive citizens. Did we understand this?

During his little speech to us, I felt my face turning red. Carol, sitting beside me, tensed up and, I knew, was about to explode. I grabbed her knee to restrain her and said sweetly "Yes, Evgeny, we understand. We will certainly respect this from now on. I am sorry we did not know the rules." I stepped outside myself again and watched as I lied to the commissar. Of course we had known the rules. What was I becoming, when I found a lie to be more beneficial than the truth?

The commissar and his slugs were extra vigilant for a few days. Then things settled back down. We returned to our life of working trawls and hanging out with the Banditos in the chi room. Tea was the strongest beverage that made its appearance from then on in our group.

A couple of weeks of normal, sea-going life went by. Valerya and I had both been knitting scarves, admiring each other's handiwork as the pieces progressed. We told each other the scarves were for our respective mothers. One evening I entered the chi room with my completed scarf wrapped in brightly colored tissue paper, not for my mother but for Valerya. I smiled as I stepped over the threshold and presented him with the package. Laughing, he opened his coat and pulled out a Pravda-wrapped packet, about the same size as mine. We each unwrapped our gifts and wound them around our necks, grinning foolishly and complimenting each other on the beautiful mufflers.

Carol and I both knew that our days on the *Malykin* were drawing to a close, as MAF had said they wanted us back after two months. We spent as much time as possible with the Banditos, savoring every moment. Our evenings were filled with laughter and music and mounds of fried *kartoshkas*. The glow of friendship surrounded us.

*   *   *

One morning I bounced happily into the chi room and Valerya was not there. He did not show up an hour later for the first trawl to be brought on. Strange—this had never happened before. After processing, back in the chi room, I asked the Banditos where he was. There was an uneasy silence, and the men all looked at one another. Finally, Mr. Slipper said he was sick.

"But do not worry, Dasha. He is not very sick. Probably he will work again tomorrow."

I couldn't believe that Valerya was so sick he wouldn't come to the deck. Something was going on. I quizzed the men. They insisted that everything was normal, Valerya was just ill.

"Maybe I will go to his cabin and take him some treats." I looked at Mr. Slipper. "Will you come with me?" Again, uneasy glances among the men. Mr. Slipper said it was best not to go to the cabin—he thought Valerya was asleep.

For the rest of the day, the mood among the Banditos was a somber one. Nothing I did could get a laugh out of them. Several times I came upon Bulichka and Mr. Slipper talking quietly off to the side of the deck.

When Carol woke up in the evening, I told her what was going on, how Valerya was "sick," and the men were acting strangely.

Usually Carol woke up slowly, but not so with this news. "I'll wager it's something to do with that bloody commissar." She sprang out of bed. "I'll keep my eyes open and see if I can find out what's up." She dressed for her work shift and hurried out the door.

Carol and I did not see each other again until the next morning, when she came in to wake me for my shift.

"So, did you find out what was wrong with the men? Are they still being strange?" I asked as I pulled on my coveralls.

"They are acting bloody strange, you're spot on about that. But no one would say a word about what's got them going. And I didn't see Valerya once." Carol shook her head.

I walked out onto the deck to be greeted by a leaden sky. It certainly fit my mood. I leaned against the deck railing, gazing out over the smooth surface of the sea, following the silver flow of water as it melted into the liquid sky. Everything felt soft and hazy. Further down the deck, I saw a man sitting on top of the nets stacked against the port railing; his back was angled toward me, so that I could barely make out his profile. I realized it was Valerya and started toward him. Something made me stop. He looked so vulnerable and alone atop that heap of nets. He had been looking out to sea; as I watched him, he dropped his head into his hands. His shoulders began shaking, and he rocked back and forth. My stomach twisted in pain. Oh, God, something was seriously wrong. Had he received bad news about his family? Had someone died? Suddenly, Valerya threw back his head and shouted—I caught his words in Russian—"I want to go home. I want my home."

I started as someone gripped my arm. It was Mr. Slipper, and he drew me toward the chi room. I tried to pull away, saying that I needed to speak to Valerya. I pointed toward him, and Mr. Slipper nodded, smiling sadly.

"Best, Dasha, for Valerya to be alone now. Please, come with me."

I asked him if someone had died—what was wrong? Mr. Slipper told me that no one had died, Valerya's family was fine. Everything was fine. Maybe Valerya was just sad, he didn't know.

I knew this was not true. I begged Mr. Slipper to tell me what was going on. He only shrugged his shoulders and said he did not know. I raced back to my cabin. Carol was doing paperwork when I burst in. Pacing the cabin, I told her what had just happened. Did she know anything—did she have any clue—as to what was wrong?

Carol laid down her pencil and looked silently at me. She said she didn't know what was wrong. "All the Banditos would say to me is 'Everything is OK,' just like they told you."

I didn't believe her. "Carol, look, we are mates. We've been through hell out here, you and me. If there's anyone I trust besides Valerya, it's you. Are you *sure* you don't know *anything* about what's going on?"

Again, Carol met my gaze steadily. Again, she said she did not have any more information than I did. I still did not believe her, but I had to accept what she was telling me.

Later that day, Valerya was back on deck and working. He greeted me eagerly and happily, and I asked him where he had been. He told me he had been sick but was better now. After processing the afternoon trawl, we all met in the chi room. The Banditos seemed normal, albeit somewhat subdued. We made *kartoshkas* and drank tea. Carol joined us, and Bulichka popped a tape into the player. Melancholy Russian folk tunes filled the air for a few minutes, then Valerya abruptly stood up and turned off the mournful music. He grabbed Carol's Madonna tape and turned the volume up high, immediately creating a different atmosphere in our tiny room.

Over the next several days, there were obvious clues that things were, in fact, not OK. Valerya gave me an envelope containing photographs I had given him of myself, as well as some Seattle shots.

"Dasha, best for you to keep these pictures. I would like to have them to remember you, but it is not good for me to keep them."

A few days later, he asked to see my language notebook that I carried everywhere with me, often inadvertently leaving it in the dining room or chi room. Everyone knew what this notebook was and would return it to me when they came across it. I gave it to

him, and he flipped open the front cover, where I had written his
address.

"Dasha, best please if you put my address somewhere else.
And, most important," he looked at me seriously, "Please do not
write to me at home. I will write to you first. When you hear from
me, it will be OK for you to write back to me."

I was shaken. I begged Valerya to tell me what had happened.
I asked him if he was in trouble. What had the commissar done?
He insisted that there was no particular problem, he was just trying
to be "safe" in general.

Within a week, we would be docking at Lyttleton, the port
near Christchurch, and Carol and I would fly back to Wellington.
Our last days with the Banditos were bittersweet ones. I felt as if
we had been through a war together, which in some sense, I suppose
we had. I had the terrible feeling that we had lost the battle.

They say adversity brings people closer together. It did for us.
Our bond could not have been stronger, our affection any greater.
Because of the unacknowledged trouble, we had a low-key, quiet
farewell party in the chi room. Valerya and I wore our scarves,
which, throughout the evening, we arranged on different parts of
our body. Valerya turned his into a turban at one point; I tried
mine out as a belt. Then we tied them together and wrapped Mr.
Slipper up like a mummy.

Valerya and I sat together into the early hours of the morning.
We talked of many things. Things that, for others, would seem
real, possible. For us, these things would never happen. But we let
the magic take over, spinning our dreams out loud, believing for
this night that our wishes might be more than just fantasy. I
described the places we would go, what we would see, when he
and his family came to visit me in the United States. He told me
that he would buy me a plane ticket, a plane ticket for around the
world, with a stop off in Africa for as long as I wanted. I recalled
stories of working on my boats in the Bering Sea, and we agreed
that we would certainly work together again, maybe up in Alaska.

Just before sunrise, I grabbed Valerya's hand and led him out to the deck railing. The wind whipped around us as the *Malykin* steamed toward Lyttleton. The sky was streaked with the palette of early morning colors, and a pink glow greeted us as we leaned on the railing, looking to the east.

"Ah, Dasha. What shall I do without you?" Valerya sighed and threw an arm around me, just as the sun burst over the horizon, a glowing orange ball that shone with the promise of warmth and strength.

* * *

The Malykin docked in Lyttleton around 11 in the morning. MAF had booked a 1:30 flight out of Christchurch for us. With the help of the Banditos, Carol and I hauled our bags out to the dock, tumbling over each other and our friends as our gear slowly took on the shape of a small mountain. Despite our laughter, my stomach had long ago turned into a knot and my chest felt as though a thousand octopus tentacles had wrapped around me and were slowly squeezing. I found it hard to breathe.

From a pay phone, Carol called a taxi. Within 15 minutes the cab pulled up beside us on the dock. The Banditos heaved our bags into the back seat and the trunk. Mr. Slipper sat on the lid of the trunk in order to get it to close. Bulichka shuffled bags around in the back seat, jamming smaller ones into the rear window ledge, trying to make room for Carol. Carol and I took turns hugging the men. Both of us were crying. My legs felt unable to support me and the octopus tentacles squeezed tighter. Valerya and I stood in front of each other for a long moment. Tears streamed down his cheeks, and he wiped his crooked nose with a sleeve. I threw my arms around him and breathed deeply of his familiar smell, rubbing my cheek against his soft and worn jacket. I heard him saying my name, over and over. Finally, we pulled apart, and I forced myself into the front seat of the taxi. Carol had already wedged herself into the back. Laughing and crying, we leaned out of the car windows, waving good-bye to our boys as the taxi driver honked his horn and drove down the dock. We didn't stop until the driver turned onto the street and we could no longer see the Banditos waving back at us.

Carol passed me a bandanna, telling me to use it and stop wiping my snotty nose on my bloody sleeve, just as she raked her own sleeve across her tear stained face. I plastered the bandanna completely across my face, wishing I could remain hidden beneath it. Carol wouldn't let me hide, however, and she grabbed my shoulder from the back seat.

She took a deep breath and said, "I have to tell you something."

I turned to look at her. Her eyes were swollen and her face red. "Valerya made me promise not to tell you this until we were off the boat. Please, you can't be pissed at me. I had to keep my promise to him."

I only knew I did not want to hear what was coming. And I knew my instinct had been accurate all along—Carol knew what had happened. Valerya had told her the whole story, after swearing her to secrecy. I suppose he was wise to do so; had I known what Carol was about to tell me, I think I would have killed him. Not Valerya, but the commissar.

Carol sagged back in her seat as she told me that two weeks ago, the commissar had summoned Valerya to his office and told him that he and the Banditos were no longer to spend time with Carol and me. Our interactions were to be severely restricted. No more hanging out together after work in the chi room, no more conversations in the corridor, no more drinking tea together. Each man would be allowed to say hello to us and no more. No other words were to be directed at us. As crew chief, Valerya would be responsible for enforcing this policy among his men. The commissar would be alerting his slugs to this new edict. They would monitor all of us to ensure that it was adhered to.

Valerya did the unthinkable. He said no to the commissar. A Soviet citizen simply did not contradict a commissar. But Valerya did. He told Evgeny that there was nothing wrong, dangerous or immoral about his crew's friendship with us. He refused to follow Evgeny's orders.

The commissar told Valerya he would give him one day to think this over. He was sure Valerya would change his mind.

Valerya was ordered to return to Evgeny's cabin the next afternoon. He had not changed his mind. Evgeny yanked Valerya's visa and work permit and radioed Moscow that he would be sent back to Russia at the next opportunity. The commissar told him he would never work at sea again and would never leave Russia, as his travel visa was permanently revoked. When he returned to Moscow, he was to report to party headquarters for further punishment.

I was doubled over in agony by the time Carol, sobbing, finished telling me this. The cabby asked me if I was all right, and I shook my head. He pulled over to the side of the road, and I opened the car door and threw up.

We made it to the airport. I felt like a zombie, going through the motions of purchasing an airline ticket, helping Carol thrust our overweight bags at a gaping counter attendant and finally boarding the plane. Carol kept asking me if I was all right and, each time, I nodded dully at her. We landed in Wellington and Carol called MAF, telling them we were too exhausted to come to the office today. We would report in tomorrow, probably mid-morning. I knew I could not go home that night, as I lived with a kiwi family, and I desperately needed to be alone. I told Carol that I would take a taxi to a nearby motel. She wanted to come with me, but I told her I had to be by myself.

"Look, I'll call you in the morning. Maybe we can get together before we go to MAF. I just need to try to sort this all out."

Carol nodded. "Just remember, Dail, you don't have to take this all on yourself. We were both there, we're both bloody responsible. It's not you alone."

*   *   *

Even six years later, as I write this, reliving the pain of the following days and weeks overwhelms me. I was consumed by loss and agonizing, crippling grief. Mostly, however, it was guilt that ate away at my very soul. I could not eat and I did not sleep. How was I to live with the fact that I had ruined a man's life? I walked, for miles, it seemed, all over the city, alone with my pain, feeling frustrated, useless and totally helpless. I sat for hours on the bench in Central Park, shivering in the wind of Wellington, staring at the sky. The agony of not knowing what was to happen to Valerya was unbearable. There must be some way I could help him. Perhaps I could lodge an official complaint with the Soviet Embassy, explaining how actions taken against Valerya were a threat to the goodwill they were working so hard to develop in their fishing program. There had been nothing dangerous or threatening in the relationship Valerya had with Carol and me. Surely I could make them see reason. My battered idealism somehow continued to push through—I wanted, still, to believe that people are basically good and will do what is right, if only they are allowed to see the injustice of a situation. Maybe it would be best to meet face-to face with officials at the Embassy and try to explain this to them.

The director of MAF simply shook his head when, several days later, after I was able to function again, I suggested this to him. "Dail, you've worked with the Soviets long enough to know better. There's not a bloody thing that you—or anyone of us—can do. Not a bloody thing. Anything we tried to do would only make it worse for him."

I knew this. I really knew this. But I did not think I could bear it. I searched for that place where my anger ran against an inner wall and broke itself into manageable pieces. I remembered this place; I had been there before. After the New Year's punishments were handed down. My anger did not consume me then; I was able, still, to breathe. But not now, not with this.

There are events in one's life where the pain is so great that only time can ease it. Nothing else will do. Only the passage of time can heal, partially, wounds that go so deep. This was that time for me. I traveled again through New Zealand, hitchhiking my way around that glorious countryside. I shared my story with no one. Who, after all, could understand it? I did not want the reaction that I knew I would receive if I tried to make someone understand what had happened. The polite nods and murmurs of, "Oh, how awful." In my chest sat a rock, a secret, silent agony, that I could not shift. There was no one, anywhere, who could carry it for me. I felt set apart from everyone around me.

I thought a lot about loyalty. And courage. The meaning of the words. The living of the words. Would I have had the courage to defy the commissar? Would I have cast off my culture, my world, my government to be loyal to something so simple, so innocent as friendship? A friendship that was destined to end anyway, Valerya and me forced apart by the simple obstacles of distance and separation.

Loyalty. To defy all reason and common sense and danger to remain true to what one values the most. What did I value the most? My family. My close friends. Valerya. Freedom. To be human, to touch another person in a real way. To feel so strongly about someone or something that I would do what Valerya had done.

Eventually I went back to work—on a Japanese ship. I would never work on a Soviet boat again. The system had succeeded in breaking me. The Russians had won, this battle that we had been through. But in its victory, it had inadvertently given me the things that it most wanted to destroy. I had experienced love and loyalty and courage, all in their most human of forms.

And I began to understand it now, this love I felt for Valerya that defied all definition. You have to believe in it, in a certain kind of collusion of the fates that allows a coming together. You have to believe that once—maybe twice—in our lifetime on this earth, we may meet someone with whom there is a spark, a flash and an instant, mutual recognition of a bond that is rare and so unique as to defy all logic. And I believed it. Because I had lived it. So perhaps, after all, I had not lost the fight.

EPILOGUE

EVENTUALLY I RETURNED TO THE UNITED STATES. FIRST, I SPENT time traveling in Australia and Indonesia. And, backpack fully loaded, I journeyed through Africa for six months. I often wished I could let Valerya know that I survived the trip and, though there were a couple of close calls, I hadn't been consumed by a hungry lion.

I kept in touch with Carol. She continued to work for MAF, and she sometimes went out on Soviet ships. Around Christmas of 1990, I got a letter from her telling me that, on one of her boats, she heard that the commissar from the *Malykin* had been murdered back in the USSR. The rumor was that some of his crewman had done it. I envisioned Bulichka, a machete in hand and a bandanna over his face, the perfect hit man. Carol's source told her the killers were uncaught. I read these words and smiled. Perhaps, after all, there was some kind of justice in this world.

* * *

In July of 1991, I began working with a Seattle-based women's health care project that planned to establish birthing centers in the Soviet Union. In August, the coup toppled the communist government of the USSR. I was stunned, as was the entire world. The break up of the Soviet Union was something I could never have imagined in my lifetime. Events in the USSR continued to unfold, clearly indicating that the communists were out of power. The health care project had planned a trip to Russia in late September, and our travel agent advised us to go ahead. On September 18, twelve of us boarded a plane to Moscow. Packed in my carry on bag was my journal with Valerya's address and phone number in it.

As we disembarked in the Moscow airport, confusion surrounded us. Like water bursting through a dam, a flood of feeling washed over me, threatening to knock me over. I breathed in the smell of Russia—and of my boats. Surrounded by hundreds of people speaking in Russian, I could have been back among my crew members.

Tania, our trip leader who was married to a Soviet, had arranged for us to be taken by van directly to the place we were staying—30 minutes outside of the city. It was an old resort that had formerly been reserved for the elite of the Communist Party. With Tania's incredible connections, she had managed to wangle us in. The promise of a good deal of hard currency from us as paying guests, I am sure, helped cement things.

Tania, who spoke excellent Russian, had promised me that she would phone the number Valerya had given me when we worked on the *Malykin*. I had decided that, with the political situation in turmoil, surely it would be safe to attempt to contact Valerya. I held little hope of actually reaching him, but I would not leave Russia without making every attempt possible.

Late that first night, an exhausted Tania tried the number. She did not get through, and shrugged at me, turning to go to bed. I begged her to try it once more, just once more. She rolled her bleary red eyes at the ceiling and sighed, dialing the number again. This time she reached an operator who told her the number had been changed. She dialed the new number. It seemed to ring for an eternity. Just as she was about to hang up, someone answered. Tania spoke rapidly for a minute, then handed me the phone, saying only "It is Valerya."

I grabbed the phone, unbelieving. I said hello in Russian, my voice shaking.

"Dasha, is it you? Is it really you? Are you here? Is it truly you?" It was Valerya's voice. We were on the Moscow telephone together.

My limited knowledge of Russian left me, and all I could do was mumble, the receiver trembling in my hand. I handed Tania the telephone and told her I needed to arrange a time to see Valerya. Could he see me?

As I sank into a chair next to the phone, Tania spoke for several minutes. I understood little of what she said. I knew a group planned to go into Moscow the next night to visit a local nightclub, and when Tania hung up, she said that is where Valerya would meet us. She had arranged the meeting time for 10 p.m.

It seemed an eternity until the next evening. I could barely get through the meetings I attended. My only thought was of seeing Valerya. Finally, after a late dinner at the resort, the taxi that Tania had called for us arrived. Only five of us were going into the city, and the entire group knew my story. The ride into Moscow seemed endless. A gentle rain was falling, and the streets shimmered under the streetlights that sporadically functioned. Tania pointed out a few sights as we chugged along, the driver going slowly to avoid gaping potholes in the road. We maneuvered into the heart of Moscow and circled Red Square. The cream colored walls of the fortress-like Kremlin shone under floodlights. The multi-colored onion domes of St. Basil's cathedral glistened under a fine sheen of water.

The taxi driver parked on the north side of Red Square, and we tumbled out, all looking in different directions. Suddenly, I felt hands over my eyes. Laughter filled my ears. I whirled around, and there he was. Valerya stood in front of me, tears streaming down his cheeks. I leaned into his arms and wrapped my own around him, sobbing with joy, relief and a thousand other feelings. The group gathered around us clapped and cheered. The lights of Red Square shone through the night.